No Hatch to Match

AGGRESSIVE STRATEGIES FOR FLY-FISHING BETWEEN HATCHES

Rich Osthoff

STACKPOLE BOOKS

0 11557 03152 2

To Dale and Dana,
whom I wouldn't have missed for the world.

Copyright © 2001 by Stackpole Books

Published by
STACKPOLE BOOKS
5067 Ritter Road
Mechanicsburg, PA 17055
www.stackpolebooks.com

Printed in the United States

10 9 8 7 6 5 4 3 2 1

First edition

Cover design by Wendy A. Reynolds
Cover and inside photos by Rich Osthoff
Fly plate photo by Paul Baker
Illustrations by Dave Hall

Library of Congress Cataloging-in-Publication Data

Osthoff, Rich
    No hatch to match / Rich Osthoff.— 1st ed.
      p.   cm.
    Includes bibliographical references (p.).
    ISBN 0-8117-3152-9 (pbk.)
    1. Flies, Artificial. 2. Trout fishing. I. Title.

SH451 .O87   2001
799.1'24—dc21

                                       2001020153

Contents

Preface

Much of the lore and literature of fly-fishing for trout revolves around matching the hatch. And with good reason. Watching the snout of a really good trout break the surface to inhale your dry fly amidst a flotilla of naturals is a singular sporting thrill. When the surface bulges right on cue and line zips from your reel at an alarming rate, it's living proof that you've made exactly the right moves in fly fishing's classic matchup.

But in reality, large trout rise to frequent and dependable hatches only on a relative handful of exceptionally fertile waters. Most days on the more ordinary trout waters that most of us fish, there is no significant hatch to bring the best trout to the surface. Even if there is such a hatch, it rarely lasts for more than a few hours. When a hatch fizzles or fails to transpire, your choices are to bag the rod, fish halfheartedly, or get resourceful.

This is a book about fishing resourcefully between hatches—a surprisingly neglected subject, considering that for most of us, it encompasses the bulk of our time on the water. Hey, hatches come and go, but it's how we use the hours and days between hatches that largely governs our angling enjoyment and success.

The term "nonhatch period" has a negative connotation that is sometimes deserved. It's true that between hatches, trout often retreat to refuge lies and develop lockjaw. But it's also a good bet that you'll bump into your largest and most aggressive trout during nonhatch periods. Why? Because usually it's an invigorating water temperature, not a hatch, that puts big predatory trout on the prowl.

Learning to fish well between hatches isn't some angling side road. It's main-street stuff you'll use every outing. It's learning to deal with tough conditions from sweltering heat to dirty water. It's mastering subtle techniques, such as micronymphing at close quarters for inactive trout, and aggressive techniques, like long-line nymphing with dry-fly precision for active trout. It's anticipating temperature-induced feeding binges and understanding the seasonal factors that govern where in a watershed the bulk of the trout will be. It's identifying niches of active trout and then covering water at a productive clip to exploit those niches. It's having some parlor tricks up your sleeve and recognizing opportunities to use them. It's learning from other anglers and solving some riddles on your own.

This is also a book about fishing ambitiously. I know, I know, fly fishing is supposed to be play, not work, but like most anglers, I have a heck of a lot more fun when I fish well than when I fish poorly. And learning to fly fish well on a variety of trout waters in an array of conditions happens only with experience, observation, and effort. Every highly skilled angler I've met is a bit driven, at least when it comes to fishing—that's what keeps them on the water and advancing through the lean times as well as the gravy times.

Of course, fly-fishing for trout is about more than the number of fish brought to net. It's about the Montana sun on your shoulders after a three-year absence, the music of the upper Madison mingling with sleep, and ice on your tent fly in August. It's silver skeins of storm sweeping off the Gravelly Range and pummeling you with hail as you huddle in the streamside willows, then glancing up to witness a storybook rainbow arching over perfectly sculpted river terraces. It's the pull of big country and pilgrimages to famed rivers and feeling expansive again. And it's Sunday mornings on local creeks that few anglers will ever hear of.

To me, the techniques and the intangibles of fly-fishing for trout are equally alluring. Fish often, fish smart, fish hard, and savor every day in trout country. I can't think of a recipe for wringing more from our allotted days on the water.

Rich Osthoff
October 2000

PART ONE

Taking
What the Water
Will Give You

Chapter 1

Anticipating Temperature-Induced Feeding Binges

Trout are cold-blooded creatures. Their activity level is governed largely by temperature. Invigorating water temperatures will move trout out of refuge lies and onto feeding stations even when there's no corresponding hatch. In fact, over a season I catch many more trout during temperature-induced feeding periods than I do during hatches, and temperature is usually the major factor in determining when, where, how, and even if I fish.

Trout are most active at water temperatures right around 60 degrees Fahrenheit. That's when their metabolisms hit high gear and their energy demands soar. That's when they feed most frequently, most aggressively, and for the longest duration. Optimal temperature varies somewhat by species and habitat. Brown and rainbow trout are generally most active at slightly above 60 degrees. Trout that are native to northern latitudes or high altitudes (cutthroats, brook trout, and golden trout) are most active at or just below 60 degrees.

Of course, trout have energy requirements throughout the year, so they feed minimally at temperatures well outside of their optimal range. By understanding how trout respond to temperature, you can anticipate major and minor feeding periods year-round.

Let's look at the effects of water temperature on trout activity in midwestern streams that experience four distinct seasons.

WINTER

For most of my youth, trout season on my home streams in southwestern Wisconsin opened in late spring, so fishing in the dead of winter wasn't an option. Then, from the mid 1970s through the late 1980s, several southwestern counties adopted a New Year's Day opener. A typical opener saw the hillsides blanketed with a foot or more of snow. January is the coldest month in Wisconsin. We usually see a string of nights when temperatures dip to 20 degrees below zero and days when the mercury struggles to top zero. A cold snap like that ices over everything but the riffles and water that's close to springs.

A few anglers made it a tradition to fish trout on New Year's Day come hell or hard water. If it was brutally cold, they actually spent most of the day in their cars nursing mugs of hot coffee and talking about fishing, but at some point they officially wetted a line. I fished periodically in those winter seasons, but when snow glistens knee-deep on the hillsides and afternoon temperatures top out in the single digits, I'd rather chase grouse than trout. Plowing through snow with a shotgun is so invigorating that the cold can be beaten back and even relished. By comparison, standing around in a stream amplifies extreme cold. The fish aren't all that fired up about it either—even big trout fight sluggishly. But if you need your fly-fishing fix when it's cold enough to form permafrost in your shorts, there are strategies for consistently catching some trout.

For starters, sleep late and eat a big breakfast. Winter trout are least active at daybreak, when stream temperatures bottom out—usually in the mid- to upper thirties, depending on weather and stream type. In winter, the early bird gets mostly frozen appendages and ice in the guides.

Don't automatically drive to your favorite summer haunts. Concentrate on streams that are relatively ice-free. Wide-open water indicates a proximity to springs, and in winter significant spring flows mean relatively warm water and more active fish. Large springs moderate stream temperature to a greater degree and for a greater distance than small springs do. In southwestern Wisconsin, we're blessed with dozens of small to modest-sized spring creeks that flow from limestone formations, but few of these streams emerge full-blown from a single source. Instead, most creeks have numerous small springs in their upper watersheds, plus scattered spring holes and spring tributaries in their middle to lower reaches. Most springs flow year-round at about 50 degrees. Stream temperature at any given location depends on air temperature, the volume of spring flows, and the distance from springs, but many northern spring creeks maintain nighttime temperatures of nearly 40 degrees and remain mostly ice-free in winter. Forty degrees might sound cold, but it's significantly warmer than northern freestone streams, which regularly freeze over from bank to bank and develop destructive anchor ice as the slow water along the bottom freezes. In general, the greater the volume of spring flows, the warmer a stream remains in winter. Sizable spring creeks also have deep, slow refuge runs where winter trout congregate. Water that is relatively warm, deep, and slow—that's what you're seeking in winter.

In cold weather, when their energy requirements are low, trout can find sufficient food without leaving refuge water, so feeding and resting locations are often one and the same. Sluggish winter trout won't move very far or very fast to intercept prey, so winter isn't a time to fish aggressively or to cover a lot of water. It's a time to gear down and probe deep refuge areas with a slow presentation at the exact level of the fish. On the plus side, trout in refuge lies are often bunched. If you hook a winter fish, stay put and replicate your drift precisely, because you may be able to run several fish from your position.

Even moderate winter days are preceded by long, cold nights. It's usually late morning before the air warms significantly and water temperature climbs a couple notches. Sunlight can boost water temperature even on subfreezing days, so stick to exposed meadow streams when the sun is out. In winter, it only takes a bump of a few degrees to stimulate feeding. However, winter days are short and the sun crests at a low angle, so daytime gains in water temperature are short-lived. Make it a point to be on the water when temperatures peak—from noon to about 3 P.M. Eating a late breakfast fuels you right through the peak fishing hours without having to break for lunch.

In winter, it's an advantage to fish on a day that's warmer than the preceding day, because trout and prey activity will be on the increase. If the forecast is for marginal temperatures, the direction of temperature is especially critical. A 35-degree day following a 25-degree day usually trig-

Inactive Trout Positions. Inactive trout typically bunch in slow, deep refuge water where they're secure from predators and can hold with minimal effort.

gers some significant midday feeding. A 35-degree day following a 45-degree day usually means slow fishing.

Not surprisingly, the best winter fishing usually coincides with unseasonably mild weather. Forty-five-degree days followed by comfortable nights allow daytime water temperatures to climb into the lower forties, causing trout to feed more actively and to expand their midday feeding window a bit. If a winter thaw triggers heavy snowmelt, then water temperatures will be depressed on streams that receive heavy runoff, and the fishing will shut down. But if a chinook arrives to find very little snowpack, or if warm weather lasts beyond the period of heavy snowmelt, the stage is set for a few days of fast winter fishing.

That's exactly what happened in the winter of 2000 in southwestern Wisconsin. A thaw in late February blew out our snow in less than a week and just in time for our March catch-and-release season. As streams dropped and cleared during the first week of March, we basked under sunny skies and record warmth. On my first outing of the millennium, on March 6, the air warmed to 75 degrees and I fished in shirt sleeves. When I began fishing at 11 A.M., the water temperature was already 45 degrees. I stuck my first fish almost immediately—a 16-inch brown that launched from under a cutbank to whack a Soft-Hackle Woolly Bugger. Just after I set the hook, I saw the trout disgorge a 6-inch chub—a sure sign that this was a hungry fish. The day only got better. Action really picked up around noon, when the water temperature hit 48 degrees. From 2 P.M. until the sun dropped behind the hills at 5:30, the water hovered at an incredible 52 degrees—easily the warmest I've ever experienced in Wisconsin for that date. Aggressive browns were all over the drink. I tossed small Woolly Buggers all day, and on nearly every good-looking run I caught several fat browns. My biggest fish of the day, an 18-inch hen, moved a good 4 feet to intercept a bugger just after it hit the water. That winter day produced the kind of hard-charging trout that I usually don't see in Wisconsin until well into April—and their hunger was strictly temperature induced, as hatch activity was limited to a few midges. Within a few days, however, we were jolted back to reality by wet snow and daytime highs in the twenties.

SPRING

For trout anglers, spring is the season of greatest transition. Stark winter conditions can prevail well into March, but by the end of May, a scant two months later, the woods and fields are in full bloom, and the first blasts of summer heat arrive. In between, you'll encounter the most invigorating water temperatures and the most aggressive trout of the year. In Wisconsin, our general trout season opens the first Saturday in May, but we have catch-and-release fishing in March and April. For productive midday fishing, I wouldn't swap April for any other month.

In the Midwest, snow has usually melted from all but the shaded hollows and north slopes by early April. Nights often dip below freezing, resulting in cold water and inactive trout at daybreak, but with the longer days and the higher angle of the sun, the water warms quickly into the midforties on most mornings. In early spring, midday is still the best time to fish, but by the end of April, the window of favorable water temperatures widens to include most of the daylight hours. As daytime water temperatures climb into the midfifties, trout not only feed more aggressively, but begin to fight with real vigor. They jet around pools with alarming speed and surge for protective cover with surprising power. By late April, you can have your hands full landing the same trout that came meekly to heel in the cold water of winter and early spring.

Spring weather systems import rain, which can elevate water temperatures at any time. The first mild, rainy days of spring are super days to be on the water, even at dawn. In fact, at any season or time of day, rain almost always moves water temperature toward the comfort zone for trout and stimulates feeding activity. Unlike snowmelt, rain also boosts oxygen levels, which helps invigorate the trout. Spring rains come at a time when a lot of aquatic insects are nearing emergence—that sudden bump in both water temperature and stream flow usually puts a lot of vulnerable organisms in the drift. Be there if you can.

In spring, the intensity of evening trout activity depends on how rapidly the air, and subsequently the water, cools. On a crisp, clear evening, warmth radiates quickly into the atmosphere, and feeding slows dramatically in late evening. On mild, overcast evenings, water temperature drops slowly, and trout may feed aggressively right into dark. As a rule, if the evening air feels soft, it should pay to fish late.

Throughout spring, the fishing steadily improves as the water warms, but spring is never a straight-line progression. On a 45-degree day following a 70-degree day, both fish and insect activity are sharply reduced, but on the very next warm day, activity rebounds quickly. In spring, it pays to remain flexible with some of your fishing time rather than schedule everything in advance, because you can encounter cold or mild weather on any given day.

As spring advances and trout metabolisms rev up, the fish continue to rest in deep or protected water just as they did in winter, but to feed, they move to prime feeding stations—usually in shallower or more open water— where they can efficiently capture more food. In the Midwest, many of our best caddis and mayfly hatches occur in April and May, but regardless of

Active Trout Positions. Feeding trout typically disperse throughout a run to relatively shallow feeding stations, including those at the head and tail of a pool and along its banks.

whether there's a hatch, invigorating water temperatures often cause trout to gravitate to feeding stations by midmorning and remain on the prowl for much of the day. That makes spring a great time to fish banker's hours and to run and gun with a prospecting fly between hatches. Later we'll look at techniques, including long-line nymphing, that let you cover water quickly and efficiently as you prospect for aggressive trout.

SUMMER

When midday water temperatures climb into the mid-60s, a reversal takes place in trout behavior. Instead of feeding at midday, trout begin to concentrate their feeding toward the margins of daylight, when water temperatures are close to optimal. For much of the day, trout retreat to deep or shaded refuge lies and become less active. Hooking lethargic summer trout requires the same slow, precise, subsurface presentations that are needed for sluggish winter trout.

In summer, overcast skies often produce some of the best daytime fishing. Even if a big hot-air mass is in place, cloud cover moderates air temperature and reduces solar heating of the water. Clouds also reduce fish-spooking shadows, making trout feel more secure and encouraging a shift from deep refuge lies to shallow feeding stations.

With luck, it may even rain. Summer showers can lower water temperature and boost oxygen levels enough to trigger significant trout activity. Summer rains also wash a lot of terrestrial insects into streams. If light-ning isn't a danger and heavy rains don't turn the water to chocolate, you might see the type of unselective feeding frenzy you haven't seen since the optimal water temperatures of spring.

As July advances, trout in warm stream sections begin to feed primar-ily at night. In early summer, water temperatures typically drop into the mid- to lower sixties shortly after sundown, so by extending your fishing even an hour into darkness, you'll often catch a flurry of activity. By the dog days of August, temperatures may not drop enough to trigger sub-stantial feeding activity until close to dawn, so you're better off hitting the water before daybreak rather than fishing far into night.

As summer settles in and water temperatures in the deeper refuge areas begin to hover above the comfort zone of trout for most of the day, wild trout migrate in search of more comfortable conditions. Some trout seek broken water with a higher oxygen content, which makes high tem-peratures more tolerable, but most fish seek cooler water. Scattered spring-cooled runs in middle to lower watersheds attract concentrations of summer trout. But many trout migrate significant distances upstream into spring-cooled tributaries and headwaters. Various other seasonal factors cause trout to migrate within watersheds, but for much of the summer, trout anglers can stay in contact with reasonably active daytime trout by following them upstream.

AUTUMN

Autumn, with its dwindling daylight and cool nights, lowers water tem-peratures and reinvigorates the trout. As algae blooms die off and weed growth recedes, streams take on an inviting clarity that is bittersweet, since trout season is ending in many places. As water temperatures drop, trout revert to their springtime pattern of feeding most aggressively at midday. On a crisp football Saturday, a typical midwestern trout stream doesn't warm into the midfifties until early afternoon, but once the water warms, I often experience the kind of midday action I haven't seen since late spring. If a fall evening has a soft, summerlike feel, you can bank on fast fishing right into last light, but if it's cool and crisp, activity usually drops sharply before dark. Daybreak fishing is relatively slow unless the weather is unseasonably warm or a mild rain boosts water temperature.

By mid-September, fall spawners, such as brown and brook trout, are sporting radiant spawning colors and are pushing upstream toward firm spawning gravel. Spawning movement, coupled with the fact that many trout head upstream in summer in search of cooler water, means that headwaters definitely bear watching as the season winds down.

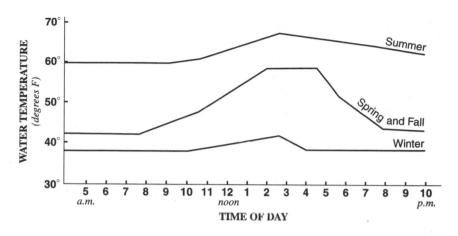

These seasonal temperature patterns are typical of many trout waters.

Through most of autumn, terrestrial insect populations remain strong, and multibrooded aquatic insects, such as *Baetis* mayflies, reappear. Although temperatures are similar in spring and fall, by autumn trout are more conditioned to looking up for their food than they were in spring. Many anglers look forward to autumn for its excellent streamer fishing, but this is also one of the best times to stick a top-end trout while prospecting with a substantial dry fly like a hopper or cricket.

Just as you did in spring, adjust your tactics to the activity level of the trout. If active trout are on shallow feeding stations, throw a long line to avoid spooking fish, and hit each likely station with just a cast or two. If trout are inactive and hunkered in deep water, stalk close and work them methodically with a short line.

In autumn, prespawn brook and brown trout become territorial and attack brightly colored flies out of sheer aggression. You don't have to fish gaudy steelhead patterns, but adding some pop to your flies can tick off some big fish. In September, I sometimes retire my favorite prospecting nymph, a Soft-Hackle Woolly Worm in black and grizzly, in favor of an all black one with a hot orange tail of soft, seductive rabbit fur. The effect can be something like waving a red bandanna in front of a juiced-up bull.

UNIQUE HABITATS

Large spring creeks are unique fisheries that shrug off many of the effects of extreme climate. Big-time spring creeks that emerge full blown from major springheads, like those of the Paradise Valley in Montana, produce remarkably stable fishing and dependable hatches year-round—even when the snow is piled high. In winter, it's relatively easy to get on the famous western spring creeks that are booked solid in summer. But be forewarned, your home waters may look like chopped liver forever after. A friend of mine went to Livingston to fish the Yellowstone spring creeks some fifteen winters ago—and he's still there.

The best tailwater rivers function like giant spring creeks, making them excellent destinations when much of the country is gripped by cold or heat. Their dams release cool water year-round from the middepths of reservoirs. Premier tailwaters, like the San Juan in New Mexico and the Green in Utah, support incredible numbers of trout with phenomenal growth rates that are rarely rivaled under natural conditions. As much as I seek solitude in my angling, I have to admit that fishing the best tailwaters when they're really rocking is as much pure fishing fun as I've had. (In chapter 14, I discuss strategies for finding elbow room on popular tailwaters even when the tourist crunch is on.)

Waters at high elevations or far northern latitudes remain cool throughout summer, making them attractive late-summer destinations when most trout waters around the country are running tepid. Over the past twenty-five years, I've made well over a hundred backpacking trips to fish wilderness waters throughout the Rockies in mid- to late summer. Near or above timberline, the biggest fish live almost exclusively in lakes, not streams, and many high lakes are under ice for better than nine months a year. Following a rough winter, I once trekked to a favorite brook trout lake atop the Beartooth Plateau in Montana to find big rafts of ice drifting about and 37-degree water in the shallows—in August. Alpine lakes tend to remain so cold right through the brief mountain summer that heat and sunlight become an angler's allies. I often experience my best high-lake fishing on warm, sunny summer days when heat activates the food chain and trout invade the shallows to feed under ideal sight-casting conditions.

Throughout the low and moderate elevations of the West, daytime air temperatures can sizzle in summer, but cool nights, cold feeder streams tumbling from the mountains, and short mountain summers combine to suppress water temperatures on many valley streams and rivers. Often in August, I've fished western river valleys when the air temperature was well above 90 degrees but the water temperature remained near an optimal 60 degrees all day long.

A TEMPERATURE GAME PLAN

Fish local waters every weekend possible while daytime temperatures are favorable. Make whatever trade-offs you can on the home front to free up prime April and May weekends. (Hey, you don't mind changing diapers, anyway.) Use personal time, sick time, or the Family Medical Leave Act to free up a few gorgeous weekdays in spring—it's a special treat to fish local waters when they're really clicking and nobody else is around. When local fishing tails off in late summer or closes in winter, use the bulk of your vacation to travel to habitats that fish well year-round or to where the seasons are reversed.

For most of us chumps, there are years when destination fishing just isn't in the cards. We either fish locally right through the tough times or sock the rod. Those are years when playing the temperature card adroitly can mean some pretty solid fishing that takes the sting out of not quite making it to the Rockies or New Zealand.

Chapter 2

Tracking Seasonal Trout Movement

Wild trout that aren't blocked by beaver dams, waterfalls, or man-made obstacles often migrate significant distances in search of comfortable water temperatures, suitable spawning habitat, or abundant forage. Most long-range trout movement is seasonal and predictable, and anglers who can anticipate where the bulk of the trout will be in a given watershed have a leg up in actually finding them.

Much of what I know about seasonal trout movement I first observed on Wisconsin streams, but as I've fished more widely, I've confirmed that trout in other regions often migrate in response to the same seasonal factors. The general principles covered in this chapter apply to many watersheds throughout the country.

BROWN TROUT

Think of a stream or river in your region that supports wild, stream-bred trout of a couple pounds or larger. Regardless of where you live, chances are you're thinking about brown-trout water. As logging, farming, industry, and urban sprawl have warmed, polluted, and silted most of our moving water, the imported brown trout has often filled the void left by retreating natives such as brook trout and cutthroats. Browns are able to thrive and reproduce in somewhat degraded habitats and are more difficult to catch than other trout, which increases the odds that they'll survive long enough to reproduce.

Brown trout are autumn spawners. Throughout the country, most browns spawn in October and November. By then, trout season is closed in much of the East and Midwest, so many anglers don't pay much attention to migration patterns. That's a mistake, because most large streams in the eastern half of the country warm to uncomfortable summer temperatures, and browns often begin their upstream movement in summer as they seek cooler water. A string of hot days with afternoon water temperatures approaching 70 degrees triggers significant upstream movement. Some fish will move into cooler tributaries. Others stay within main stems and simply move upstream. By fishing higher in watersheds as summer progresses, you accomplish two things: You stay in contact with the bulk of the brown trout in a stream system, and you fish relatively cool waters where browns are still reasonably active in daylight.

Summer movement isn't necessarily long-range. Browns stop wherever they find tolerable temperatures. That could be the bottom of an exceptionally deep pool that remains 2 degrees cooler than the upper levels of a stream. Many large streams have scattered pools that are cooled by springs welling out of their streambeds, and each summer these major springholes attract and concentrate trout. In summer, some opportunistic browns take up temporary residence just downstream from tiny spring tributaries that flow into main stems. By moving only a short distance, some trout find microenvironments that allow them to spend the summer in otherwise tepid water. Observant anglers who discover and remember these spots can usually pound up a few hot-weather trout when the rest of a stream turns off.

September afternoons often can be summerlike, but the days are getting shorter. As the nights lengthen and cool, browns begin to display their coppery spawning hues, and they move upstream. In the Midwest and the East, hook-jawed browns suddenly start showing up in tight headwaters that demand stealth and creative casting. Now you have a legitimate shot at landing a bragging-size brown on a stream you can broad-jump. Until spawning actually begins, big trout loiter where they feel most secure—in the deepest depressions or under logs, boulders, or cutbanks. In small headwaters, secure refuge cover is scarce, so choice lies can attract good fish each autumn. Where you catch or see a big brown late in the season, that's a spot you want to check the following fall.

In the valley rivers of the Rockies, browns spawn mainly in October and November, but many migrations get under way in September. In large river systems, browns may migrate many miles. Some browns that spawn in the headwaters of Montana's small Ruby River spend most of the year in the Jefferson or Beaverhead River. The abundant 5-pound browns that spawn in the headwaters of the Wind River above Dubois, Wyoming, spend the summer in large water dozens of miles downstream. The West also has many cold-water lakes and reservoirs that harbor browns that run up rivers to spawn. Hebgen Lake near West Yellowstone is famous for big browns that ascend the upper Madison River to spawn in Yellowstone Park.

In the sparkling flows of the Rockies, browns sometimes spawn successfully right in big, main-stem rivers. But in most of the country, they must migrate to headwaters to find the clean gravel and cool, stable flows needed for successful egg incubation. Since small headwaters lack the cover or forage to sustain many adult trout, postspawn browns usually drop downstream to winter. That puts the bulk of wild adult browns in middle to lower watersheds in spring, when trout seasons open in most regions, and sets up ideal conditions for targeting trophy browns with big prospecting nymphs and streamers.

In most watersheds, as you move downstream from quality to marginal trout habitat, you reach a point where trout density drops sharply. But don't quit fishing there—especially in spring on brown trout water—because just below, where trout density falls off the table, trout size often increases dramatically. Degraded downstream sections, with their collapsed banks and silted runs, never attract a lot of browns, but they have scattered holding water and remain cool enough for browns right into early summer. And lower watersheds are usually stuffed with chubs, shiners, and minnows for predatory browns to gorge on. Abundant baitfish coupled with light angling pressure gives nomadic browns that venture downstream an excellent crack at growing large.

In southwestern Wisconsin, I take most of my 20-inch browns while fishing lower watersheds on warm spring days. I usually have a lot of water to myself, because if it looks like sucker water from the bridges, few anglers will explore it ambitiously enough to discover the scattered holding lies. Of course, where trout densities are thin, you need favorable conditions to move worthwhile numbers of fish. That's why spring is ideal for exploring downstream sections. Water temperatures hover in the fifties much of the day, and trout are so aggressive that they'll pound a big nymph or streamer on the first presentation. You can fling a big fly that appeals to big fish and is readily seen, and you can fish fast and cover a lot of water. You may need to run a mile or more of stream to hook a trout, but when you do, it's likely to be a mature fish that makes you forget about the pods of smaller trout upstream.

During heat waves, browns can tolerate a few afternoons when water temperatures reach 80 degrees or slightly higher, but they live mainly where summer water temperatures rarely exceed 75. Since lower watersheds are farthest from the moderating influence of springs, they're the first to warm to uncomfortable levels in summer, and their trout are the first to start moving up a system. In southwestern Wisconsin, we usually see that kind of movement in July. In a small watershed, a big brown may only have to move two miles upstream from its springtime foraging haunts to find suitable summer temperatures. In autumn, that same fish may swim only another mile upstream to spawn successfully. In small stream systems, seasonal trout migrations are short-range and don't involve hundreds of fish moving in unison, but they're still important to anglers.

Thirty years ago, beaver were rare in southern Wisconsin, but dams now plug many streams. Dams are good news for wood ducks, but they prevent brown trout from ranging freely within a watershed and using all of their niches. Big browns in lower watersheds are blocked from reaching spawning habitat, and juvenile browns hatched in headwaters can't navigate downstream to areas of abundant forage. When dams remain intact for several years, the result is often two isolated trout populations: a dense population of small browns in the headwaters, and a modest or declining population of larger browns in the lower watershed. When you encounter a beaver dam, especially in autumn, probe the first good runs below the dam, because mature browns that are thwarted from running upstream in search of cooler water or spawning habitat will hold there.

The imported brown trout is better suited than any native trout to living in developed regions. Without browns, we'd have few top-notch wild-trout fisheries in the East and Midwest and far fewer in the West. The introduction of an exotic species is not always a bad thing.

BROOK TROUT

Brook trout are fall spawners; over much of their range, they spawn at about the same time as brown trout. In fact, in Wisconsin, I catch an occasional tiger trout—a rare, wild cross between a brook and a brown. Brook trout do require colder, cleaner water than browns. They thrive mainly where water temperatures rarely exceed 65 degrees. Brookies are also easily decimated by angling pressure. Throughout their native U.S. range— the East, the upper Midwest, and the Appalachians—brookies now find cold water and solitude primarily in small, wooded headwater streams, where they rarely grow large.

In presettlement times, brook trout of impressive proportions dominated many sizable streams and rivers from Maine to the Great Lakes. Early settlers in southwestern Wisconsin commonly caught brook trout of several pounds from streams that are now dominated by browns. Today a brook trout topping a pound is an extraordinary trophy from those same waters. On the bright side, as habitat improves in some Wisconsin watersheds, brookies are expanding their range downstream, and I'm regularly catching fish that top a foot in length, with an occasional brookie to 16 inches. Perhaps in my lifetime, brook trout of several pounds will again thrive in some of my home waters.

Many midwestern watersheds have solid populations of brook trout in their headwaters but are dominated by brown trout in their middle and lower reaches. In spring, when the water is cool, I catch a mix of browns and brookies in the middle sections of certain streams. By late June, those same sections produce mostly browns. The brookies have already moved upstream to cooler, shaded headwaters where casting is so obstructed that just putting a fly on the water often calls for a bow-and-arrow cast, a downstream drift, or dapping. Not many anglers will brave biting bugs and lush foliage to fish woodland brookies in summer, but those who do find that the fishing remains pretty consistent in cool headwaters right through the dog days of August. You can also take advantage of the brookie's cold-loving nature on nippy spring days when water temperatures are marginal for brown trout activity, say 44 degrees. On such days, I often head for brook-trout water and encounter relatively active fish.

Headwater streams usually have a few sizable runs where conventional fly casting is possible. These bigger runs hold good numbers of fish throughout summer, and prespawn brookies really gravitate to them. I have a favorite brook trout stream where I usually close out the Wisconsin trout season in late September. By then, the bottom of one deeply scoured pool is blackened by the ebony dorsals of dozens of staging brookies—solid adult fish of 10 to 15 inches. When brought to hand, an autumn brookie smolders with an unmatched palette of bold and subtle hues. To my eye, there's no more beautiful trout (OK, char), and I've caught hundreds of brilliantly colored golden trout. When I fish for brookies on neglected headwaters, I fish for all the right reasons—for the cathedral quiet of the deep woods, for the shimmer of crystalline headwaters, and for trout that are flawless in color and form. If I had only one day left to fish, I just might settle for a brook trout stream in Indian summer.

Most of the brook trout I catch that are measured in pounds, rather than inches, come from lakes in the high Rockies. Brookies aren't native to the West, but they were introduced widely before 1950, and scores of mountain waters are now overpopulated with stunted fish. Finding big brookies among the clouds is a game of exploring for lakes that have low fish densities and abundant forage (often freshwater shrimp). New beaver ponds are fertile, stillwater habitat where brookies have a shot at growing large. Mountain lakes that winterkill periodically can produce nice fish during a string of mild winters. Some high lakes that lack natural reproduction recruit a few brookies through stream systems during high flows, and those trout can quickly balloon to impressive girths while feeding in solitude. I've stumbled upon a few mountain lakes that are so fertile that they produce loads of 2-pound and bigger squaretails, but usually hefty high-country brookies occur where fish densities are very low. Under-standing how brook trout respond to seasonal factors is often the key to quickly locating them in low-density lakes.

Ice-out is prime time. Above timberline, most lakes thaw in July. Brook trout, as well as other species, immediately gravitate toward the first bands of water to warm a bit. Often I spot ice-out brookies sunning just under the surface over deep water or in calm shallows.

If you know a lake that holds a few hard-to-locate trophy brook trout, autumn is another time to cash in. Falling water temperatures invigorate brookies, encouraging them to feed in shallow water, where they're easily spotted. Above timberline and in northern states, prespawn brookies begin staging off the mouths of spawning creeks by early September, and work-ing a streamer where current extends into a lake can reveal good fish. Brook trout attack baitfish imitations just as fiercely as browns do, especially in autumn, when spawning-class fish become territorial and aggressive.

CUTTHROAT TROUT

The story of the western cutthroat trout parallels that of the eastern brook trout. Both species require exceptionally cold, clean water; cutthroats, like brookies, thrive mainly where water temperatures rarely exceed 65 degrees. Both species tend to strike eagerly and are easily overharvested, not because they're inherently dumber than other trout, but because they often inhabit high-gradient or low-fertility waters, where they must strike aggressively or go hungry. Consequently, both species have been extirpated from much of their native range by decades of environmental degradation and overharvest.

Fortunately for cutthroats, pristine conditions still exist on some siz-able Rocky Mountain rivers. The Yellowstone River is the biggest and most fertile. Several miles of smooth, meadow water below the outlet of the huge Yellowstone Lake are loaded with 2- to 4-pound cutts that move freely between the lake and the river. Yellowstone Lake is the largest, most productive cutthroat fishery in the West, yet as a stillwater fishery sur-rounded by storied rivers, it's all but ignored by fly fishers. Cutthroats are spring spawners, and each June, thousands of hefty cutts from the lake surge upriver to spawn in the upper Yellowstone and its major tributaries, including Thorofare Creek. After spawning, the fish linger and feed in moving water for a few weeks as they drop back to the lake. I like to back-pack deep into the Thorofare country of the Teton Wilderness in early July, when spawning is winding down, but plenty of big, hungry cutts still remain in the headwaters some 20 miles above the lake. Action is phe-nomenal for black-spotted Yellowstone cutts that run 16 to 20 inches, and angling pressure is light on dozens of miles of large backcountry streams.

Fine-spotted westslope cutthroat once dominated most of the major westward-flowing rivers of the Rockies. The South Fork of the Flathead in northern Montana and the Middle Fork of the Salmon in central Idaho are still great cutthroat rivers in their wilderness reaches. Idaho has used catch-and-release regulations to rebuild cutthroat populations and boost fish size on fairly accessible rivers like Kelly Creek and the upper St. Joe River.

On most westslope rivers, cutts move into the headwaters or tributaries to spawn in May or June, and they remain relatively high in drainages until water temperatures begin to drop in autumn. Then the bulk of the fish head downstream to winter in big water. Cutts from Kelly Creek winter in deep pools in the Clearwater River, and cutthroat harvest on some Idaho rivers ends in mid-September to protect schooling fish.

As the native trout of the Rockies, cutts have been introduced to many naturally barren alpine lakes that now have self-sustaining populations. High-lake cutts usually spawn in inlet streams in July, and I've seen fish climb tiny, stair-step rivulets to spawn several hundred feet above lakes. Large inlet streams can host heavy spawning runs of high-lake cutts and give alpine anglers a rare crack at sizable trout on moving water. (After spawning is completed, most trout that remain in high-altitude streams are juvenile fish or are stunted adults that reside year-round in moving water.)

During the short mountain summer, lakes remain so cold that cutts, as well as other trout, may forage in the shallows all day long. In fact, fishing is often best at midday, when sunlight warms the shallows into the fifties and activates the food chain. Toward the end of an extremely hot August, alpine trout may vanish into lake depths at midday, but by early September, cooling water temperatures have cutts prowling the shallows again.

RAINBOW TROUT

Rainbows are native to the far western United States, but they've been transplanted throughout the country. Many self-sustaining populations have been established in Rocky Mountain rivers. The Madison, the Henry's Fork of the Snake, and the Upper Missouri are native cutthroat rivers that are now famous for their wild rainbows. In the East and Midwest, hatchery rainbows are dumped in many streams for put-and-take fishing, but relatively few populations of wild rainbows have been established east of the Missouri.

Rainbows have powerful migratory impulses. Bows that have access to saltwater or coldwater lakes will forage in stillwater and return briefly to their home rivers to spawn. West-coast steelhead runs are in decline, but rainbows from the Pacific still migrate more than 700 miles inland, via the Columbia and Snake Rivers, to spawn in the Clearwater and Salmon drainages of central Idaho. Introduced strains of migratory rainbows are flourishing in the Great Lakes. I caught my biggest rainbows—fish in excess of 10 pounds—from Lake Michigan tributaries while I was living in heavily populated southeastern Wisconsin between Milwaukee and Chicago. For sheer numbers of hookups, the area has world-class steelheading, but I never adjusted to fishing in urban settings. One Easter morning, while fishing in a deserted city park, I had to hastily ford a river to elude a pair of seedy characters who cased me during a couple of slow drivebys. Wisconsin has more picturesque steelheading on small streams on the Door County Peninsula and on the famed Brule River, which empties into Lake Superior. The Brule has been hosting runs of wild steelhead for more than a century. Michigan also has several large steelhead rivers with wild fish, but most Great Lakes runs are dependent on stocking. Runs are heaviest in spring, and they kick into high gear when rains warm rivers into the midforties and raise water levels enough for fish to scoot across beachheads. Some rivers, like the Brule, also host fall-run steelhead.

Rainbows that reside year-round in moving water usually spawn in spring. Like cutthroats, most bows are found in upper watersheds in spring and early summer. Rainbows can actually tolerate slightly higher temperatures than browns, but they don't adapt as well to silted or marginally polluted waters. In rivers that hold both species, rainbows often proliferate in the faster, rockier upper sections while browns dominate the slower, more-silted lower reaches. This division is usually sharpest in spring and early summer, before browns move toward their spawning grounds.

Big browns usually specialize in big prey, but rainbows have a knack for growing large on diminutive food forms. On fertile tailwater rivers that hold a good mix of browns and bows, such as the upper Missouri in Montana and the Green River below Flaming Gorge in Utah, big rainbows routinely porpoise for midges and tiny mayflies that large browns ignore. Whether I'm fishing on top or subsurface, I find that rainbows usually respond better than browns to size 18 and smaller flies. Due to their affinity for small food forms, rainbows tend to feed more actively than browns in full daylight, so long as water temperatures remain suitable. Where I have access to both species, as is the case in much of the West, I often pursue browns in low light and rainbows when it's bright.

GOLDEN TROUT

Goldens aren't widely distributed, but I've burned a lot of boot leather pursuing these radiant trout in their mountaintop habitats. Goldens evolved in a handful of high-elevation streams, primarily in the High Sierras of California. Stream-dwelling goldens are typically small, but when transplanted to high lakes with abundant forage, goldens grow to several pounds and become powerful, acrobatic battlers. The world-record golden of 11 pounds, 4 ounces came from Wyoming's Wind River Range in 1948. In the Wind River Range and in the Beartooths of Montana, I've caught deep-bodied goldens to 25 inches that topped 6 pounds.

Goldens are spring spawners, and they'll cross with rainbows or cutthroats, resulting in some funky hybrids. At elevations of 9,500 to 10,500 feet, where goldens typically live, spawning usually occurs in July. Lake goldens will spawn in inlet streams, but they prefer outlets. Some of the best lakes for trophy goldens have swift outlets that sweep newly hatched fry downstream, helping to limit the population in the parent lake. Even big spawners sometimes wash down outlets and can't climb back to lakes, so streams that drain trophy lakes are worth checking.

Goldens are the only trout that evolved exclusively at high altitudes. They feed with amazing efficiency in mountain waters of moderate fertility, and they can balloon to impressive girths in lakes that are covered with ice for nine months a year. Like rainbows, goldens often specialize in small food forms, including zooplankton of just a millimeter or two in length. Most lakes that produce big goldens also have scuds or freshwater shrimp.

The bulk of the organisms in high lakes live in the shallows, and that's where hungry goldens usually forage right through summer. Rocky flats attract trout because they provide stable habitat for many aquatic organisms. Some cirque lakes lack significant flats but are almost completely rimmed by shallow shelves that extend 5 to 15 yards from shore before dropping abruptly into craterlike depths. Shelves offer cruising trout the best of both worlds—the abundant food of the shallows and quick access to the security of deep water. Watch for trophy goldens cruising parallel to shore along the outside edges of shelves.

Mountain nights can dip below freezing, even in August. If you awaken to ice in your water bottle, it will probably be late morning before the sun warms the shallows into the midfifties and stimulates fish and forage activity. A good game plan is to sleep or move camp in the morning and be ready to fish in the afternoon when water temperatures peak.

The midday sun also creates ideal spotting conditions. On lakes with low fish densities, I usually hunt for individual trout from high vantages on bright afternoons. With a bird's-eye view, I can observe the feeding flats and how trout relate to them. Trout in alpine lakes often cruise established routes, and if you can unravel a few routes, you greatly increase your odds of intercepting trophy fish. Goldens typically cruise fast and close to bottom. When I spot a cruiser, I usually drop a fast-sinking scud imitation in its path. When spotting conditions are poor and I'm forced to fish blind, I usually work a scud where I've observed fish previously.

Mountain afternoons are usually windy, but as evening thermals reverse, the winds usually abate. Calm summer evenings are ideal for prospecting with dry flies—lake surfaces become glassy, and lack of wave action helps the shallows retain their midday warmth and keeps prey organisms active. Flies with palmered hackle, like the Elk Hair Caddis, skate well and create a slight wake that attracts fish from a wide radius. Prospecting for big goldens with dry flies is heart-stopping, because fish will charge from the depths to nail a fly on the surface, and in clear water you can see them coming. It takes some discipline to avoid striking prematurely.

Late in an exceptionally warm summer, goldens will vanish to lake depths for much of the day, but they'll usually invade the shallows as soon as shade hits the water. If a peak or ridge looms just to the west of a lake, evening shade can fall while several hours of daylight remain. When day-time fishing is unproductive, eat dinner early and be prepared to fish hard from late afternoon until dark. By early September, water temperatures are falling and midday fishing bounces back.

PART TWO

Prospecting Tactics and Flies

Chapter 3

Long-line Nymphing for Active Trout

When short-line nymphing, also known as high sticking, an angler wades close to the target water and holds most of the fly line off the water to prevent drag. A typical cast is made upstream and across current. As the fly drifts toward the angler, he elevates the rod to lift slack line off the water. As the nymph passes the angler and continues downstream, he lowers the rod to feed line at a steady rate and to extend the drift. Short-line nymphing minimizes fly-line contact with the water, but it's a bit of a misnomer in that it actually produces the longest possible drag-free drift. That makes short-line nymphing ideal for probing long, deep refuge runs where inactive trout stack up.

Active trout invite a different nymphing approach, because they usually abandon refuge water and disperse to shallower feeding stations. Some trout feed high in runs; others lurk in tails. Some take up stations near current seams, cutbanks, rocks, or logs; others work back eddies or just subsurface over deep water. Active trout are quick to pounce on food, but they're also quick to flee vulnerable feeding lies if they sense danger. The long-line nympher who can stand back and pick a run apart station by station will enjoy some truly explosive nymphing. Long lining is particularly well suited to thin water and spooky fish that can't be approached. That makes it my standard nymphing technique for active spring-creek trout, but it also has plenty of applications on rivers.

Long-line nymphing entails working your way upstream and firing casts to likely feeding stations from outside the cone of vision of trout. Casts of 30 to 50 feet are common, which means you have a significant amount of fly line on the water—line that will create drag in short order. That's tolerable because, just as in dry-fly fishing, you're covering a specific feeding station or two with each cast, and a drag-free float of just 5 to 10 feet is usually long enough to do the job. The same reach casts and

In short-line nymphing, the nymph drifts near bottom and almost vertically beneath the indicator. The angler stands close to the target water. The rod is elevated to lift fly line off the water and to minimize drag.

In long-line nymphing, the leader lies horizontally, as the nymph is presented to relatively shallow feeding lies. The angler casts a long line from outside the cone of vision of the trout. This places a significant amount of fly line on the water— line that will create drag in short order—but this is tolerable because you're covering just a specific feeding station or two with each cast.

slack-line casts that you use while fishing dry flies will help you combat drag while nymphing.

In long-line nymphing, you must recognize most feeding stations without visible clues from the fish. Take a moment to really look at a run before casting. Don't just fixate on the meat of a run; observe the margins. Especially look for casts and drifts that are tricky to execute—on hard-fished waters, those are the lies where fish gain the edge they need to survive to noteworthy size.

Since long-line nymphing is primarily a tactic for active trout, I cover each likely feeding station with just a cast or two, starting with the lowest stations in a run and working upstream. Aggressive trout usually strike on the first presentation, so covering a bunch of stations quickly is more productive than pounding a few. Long-line nymphing is particularly conducive to fishing fast, because you don't devote much time to stealth. On most runs, you just pull up and fire from beyond radar range.

A shift toward invigorating water temperatures will kick trout metabolisms into gear and move trout out of refuge lies and onto feeding stations, even when there's no hatch. When temperatures are in transition, watch for indications that trout are stirring. A quick strike to your nymph as soon as it touches down signals that trout are becoming aggressive. Likewise, trout smacking your strike indicator should alert you that it may be time to stop dredging the bottom in the refuge runs and to nymph more actively to feeding lies. If you suddenly start flushing trout out of tailouts or shallows as you approach runs, you know that hungry fish are dispersing from refuge water.

RIGGING

Since casts are on the long side, by nymphing standards, and must be delivered right on target to specific feeding stations, long-line nymphing is best suited to presenting light to moderately weighted nymphs. I weight most of my nymph hooks with about eight wraps of wire that's equal in diameter to the hook shank. That's sufficient weight to make a nymph punch through the surface on impact and to cover most shallow stations. For deeper or faster stations, I add one or more small split shot to the tippet about 8 inches above the fly. Adding or subtracting shot in small increments (size 5 to 9 shot) lets you quickly fine-tune nymph depth for any station. Don't be lazy and try to fish an entire stream without adjusting the weight. Constantly alter that shot arrangement as you move from run to run and encounter an array of depths and current speeds. I've found a simple trick for quickly removing smooth, round shot without damaging light tippets: Stretch the tippet taut, and use your hemostat to pinch shot

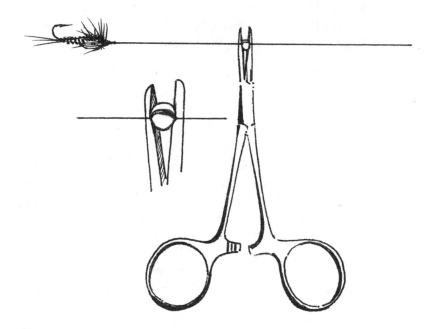

To remove round split shot, simply pull the tippet taut and pinch the shot at a right angle to the line (from the side opposite the groove). Even the smallest shot will pop open for easy removal, and it may even be reusable.

from the backside at a right angle to the groove. With a little practice, the shot will pop open and may even be reusable.

I do most of my long-line nymphing with 4-weight rods. On small streams, where accuracy is critical, I like an 8-foot rod, but on rivers, a 9-foot lets me easily extend my casting range and improves line control during the drift.

Standard rigging includes a floating fly line and an 8- to 10-foot leader with a 3X to 5X tippet. Just as in dry-fly fishing, a long leader makes it easier to avoid lining fish on upstream casts, so use the longest leader that will deliver your nymph accurately. When casting into a stiff wind, an 8-foot leader might be the longest that will deliver a weighted nymph with authority. In calm conditions or with a tailwind, you might get away with a 10-foot leader. Also use the longest tippet that you can control, because lengthening your tippet boosts its breaking strength, reduces drag, and increases the sink rate of your nymph.

Strike indicators are often derided as fly-fishing bobbers, but in long-line nymphing, the leader is extended horizontally on most drifts, and the indicator plays no role in regulating fly depth. It really is just an indicator—

a fixed point on the leader that telegraphs takes. For long lining, I usually roll a streamlined putty indicator high on the butt where it won't interfere with leader turnover. Placing your indicator close to the fly line also reduces bopping—dropping the indicator directly on top of shallow-water trout.

NYMPHS FOR LONG LINING

When long-line nymphing, I usually toss buggy, impressionistic nymphs rather than precise imitations. Hatch or no hatch, big trout often respond best to a robust nymph that offers a substantial mouthful and is easily spotted.

Nymph size is dictated by the character of the water. On big rivers, or if I'm targeting big fish, I often prospect with a big nymph, size 8 or larger. On streams, I usually prospect with a size 12 nymph. On tiny creeks or in very low water, I'll drop down to a size 16 nymph for improved accuracy and a soft presentation. On extremely fertile tailwaters, where even big fish gorge on tiny prey, I often prospect with size 18 and smaller nymphs.

My Soft-Hackle Woolly Worm in black and grizzly is my favorite prospecting nymph for many nonhatch situations. A Chocolate Hare's Ear with dark wing pads is highly suggestive of most mature mayfly nymphs (the most vulnerable kind) and is so widely effective that I rarely fish a standard Hare's Ear anymore. Scuds and sow bugs abound in fertile spring creeks, so trout get used to eating them year-round. Big freestone rivers with strong stonefly populations always hold an abundance of natural nymphs in a range of sizes.

Incidentally, long-line nymphing techniques are ideal for presenting emerger imitations during hatches. To match various mayfly emergences, I carry Rusty Floating Nymphs with dark foam wing cases in a range of sizes. They can be fished right in the film or drifted subsurface with the aid of tiny split shot. A small Bead Caddis Pupa is excellent for nymphing subsurface during caddis emergences.

CASTING

Forget the standard advice about lobbing a weighted nymph. Driving a moderately weighted nymph on a long line with dry-fly accuracy requires decent line speed.

The backcast is relaxed and deliberate—I let my hand drift well behind my ear as the backcast extends fully. The forward cast feels much like a good, crisp roll cast. Start forward smoothly and without any initial acceleration. (You want the line to be fully extended and gliding forward in preparation for the power snap.) As your hand passes your ear, chop forward and down, like you're going to bury the head of a hatchet in a stump. Stop the rod sharply a bit above horizontal. The line will surge forward like the loose contents of a minivan when you hit the brakes at high speed. For extra distance, haul downward on the forward cast and shoot extra line. For complete leader extension in a headwind or to drive a nymph on a flat trajectory, jab your elbow backward just as the forward cast straightens and the rod reaches horizontal. That transmits a secondary pulse of energy down the line that really gooses leader turnover, just as a slight reversal in hand direction causes the actual crack of a whip. A lot of long rodders grouse about the esthetics of chucking lead, but to me slinging moderately weighted nymphs on a long line is a very pleasurable form of fly casting that requires a refined casting stroke and a very precise application of power.

Long-line nymphing is station-to-station fishing. The amount of drag-free drift you get from each presentation is limited. Rather than dragging your nymph all the way back to your boots and stripping in a bunch of line that must be released through a series of false casts, make a roll-cast pickup shortly after the line begins to drag. That gets your nymph airborne and leaves you with enough line out front to load the rod with just a backcast or two, and then your nymph is right back in the water.

To me, long-line nymphing is as engaging as dry-fly fishing, and it usually produces bigger trout to boot. It's aggressive and fast paced. It places a premium on your ability to cast creatively and to read trout water. Give it a go the next time you encounter active trout on scattered feeding stations.

Chapter 4

Micronymphing
for Inactive Trout

As summer settles in and temperatures soar, trout seek refuge water for much of the day. Often they retire to the deepest slot in a run—a cool place where they can hold near bottom with little effort. Refuge slots are often quite constricted. On streams that have very little deep water, several dozen trout may stack into an area not much bigger than a bathtub. Lethargic trout won't move very far or very fast to eat, but if you drift a tiny nymph at the exact level of the fish on an absolute dead drift, you'll probably find at least a few takers.

That's the essence of micronymphing. While I do most of my micronymphing during the warm months, it's also an essential tactic for sluggish winter trout. The two main requirements are clear water and enough trout to guarantee that your tiny offerings are being seen.

FLY SELECTION
Micronymphs are sparse, natural-looking nymphs that mimic diminutive but common trout prey. I favor simple patterns that are easy to tie, in sizes 18 to 22. The Pheasant Tail Midge is my most universally effective micronymph. It employs the same materials as the popular Pheasant Tail Nymph—pheasant tail and copper wire—but I tie the midge version without legs or tails to imitate small midge and caddis larvae. Incidentally, some tailwaters, like the Green River in Utah, are loaded with dark microscuds that are too small to imitate with complex scud patterns, and the PT Midge is a simple but effective match.

The Chocolate Emerger is another superb micronymph. It imitates a small, free-swimming mayfly nymph. On midwestern streams, I fish it primarily in late spring, when trout are accustomed to seeing active *Baetis*

In micro-nymphing, the nymph is suspended vertically beneath a buoyant strike indicator and presented at the precise level of the fish. Using a buoyant indicator allows you to creep a nymph just off the bottom through even the slowest refuge runs.

nymphs. Many tailwaters are veritable *Baetis* factories that produce hatches daily over many consecutive weeks, so the Chocolate Emerger is a staple in my fly boxes when I travel.

RIGGING

Pinch just enough tiny split shot on a 5X or 6X tippet to suspend your micronymph vertically beneath a buoyant strike indicator. Then slide the indicator up or down the leader until the nymph rides at the precise depth at which trout are holding. You may need to move the indicator several times to achieve exactly the right depth. I carry a separate vial of microshot in sizes 8 and 9 so I can fine-tune my weight as conditions dictate.

For micronymphing, I favor pinch-on foam indicators, because they're small, unobtrusive, and extremely buoyant. They allow me to drift a nymph at a controlled depth through an entire run, even in current that's barely creeping. Foam indicators sit right on top of the water and wobble slightly to telegraph the lightest strikes. That's a definite advantage, because takes of micronymphs are typically very subtle, especially in slow water. When I can see fish, I watch them, rather than the indicator, for signs of a take. If a fish tips up or down, shifts laterally, or flashes its gums, I strike. With experience, you can spot a subtle take amidst a pod of fish.

PRESENTATION

Achieving an absolute dead drift is usually critical. Working at close range helps combat drag, so wade as close as you can to refuge water without scattering the fish. On shallow streams, kneeling on the bottom lowers your profile so you can get closer.

If the water has a bit of color or chop, you may be able to lay a floating line right over a pod of bottom-hugging trout without spooking them. To avoid lining trout on smooth, clear water, position yourself to cast up and across current or use a reach cast. At times, merely false-casting over fish alarms them. You can completely avoid false-casting by trailing your line downstream to load the rod, and then flicking the cast upstream.

When micronymphing, your position is critical. Moving just a few feet can eliminate subtle drag and trigger a rash of strikes. Once I locate a sweet spot where I'm getting a strike every few casts, I try to play and release fish without moving my feet so that I can replicate my drift exactly.

Some runs are a lot more vulnerable to micronymphing than others. I look for open runs with high trout densities, where the fish seek refuge in depressions on the stream bottom rather than under cutbanks, dead-falls, rocks, or other overhead structure. A choice setup is where a riffle spills into a scooped depression; the broken surface decreases the ability of trout to see above the surface, so you can stand close to the fish and work them intensively.

I've noticed that once I've micronymphed a run successfully, I can usually do it again on return visits. Over time, I've discovered a number of runs where I can consistently micronymph trout even when surrounding water is fishing poorly.

HERDING TROUT

It doesn't necessarily take extreme temperatures to bunch trout into refuge water. Fear will drive them there just as quickly. On small streams, poking your head over the bank at the wrong spot can flush fish from scattered feeding stations and send them into refuge. And it's easy to scare trout while wading or scouting unfamiliar water.

A lot of anglers just assume that spooked trout can't be caught, but I've intentionally herded wild, stream-bred browns into refuge slots and then proceeded to mop up while standing in plain view. How is that possible? Well, trout have short memories. If you stand still for a while, they forget you're there. (Herons bank on that.) More significantly, once trout have retreated to refuge water where they feel secure, they'll often tolerate your presence as long as you don't threaten them too overtly. Move slowly and give trout time to acclimate to your form, and eventually they may not associate you with a tiny nymph drifting by their snouts.

It may take fifteen minutes to settle the fish and get that first strike, but a flurry of action often follows. I'm convinced that the flashing of hooked trout can excite other trout and trigger a competitive response. Many times I've stood rooted in position for an hour and micronymphed dozens of trout from a very confined area, and the commotion of hooking and playing fish seemed to fuel the action.

MICRONYMPHING TAILWATERS

On fertile catch-and-release tailwaters, trout densities are so high that finding fish is easy. Hooking them with any consistency is the challenge. Even trout of several pounds are accustomed to grazing on small organisms, and the fish see a steady parade of anglers, so they're rarely duped by flies or presentations that don't look entirely natural. That makes micronymphing an essential tailwater tactic and a key to steady action between hatches.

On ordinary waters, I tend to micronymph when trout are inactive, because that's when they bunch into refuge lies and are easily targeted. But on tailwaters, I often micronymph even when trout are active and dispersed, because I'm still confident that fish will see my tiny nymph on most drifts. To prospect efficiently on large tailwaters, I lengthen my casts a bit and strive for very long, drag-free drifts. If I'm not hemmed in by other anglers, I move right along so that I'm constantly probing fresh water and showing the fly to different fish.

Tailwaters hold a staggering amount of trout fodder, but due to their exceptionally stable temperatures, the diversity of aquatic insect life is usually not that great. Once a given hatch begins, it's likely to occur in the same location at the same time of day for many weeks. Beneath the surface, the picture is similar, with trout chowing on heaping platters from a fairly narrow menu of midge larvae, small mayfly nymphs, scuds, and aquatic worms, which burrow into the bottom sediments of many tailwaters. A brief session of shuffling the bottom and netting samples will reveal the dominant organisms that you should be imitating. And with so many fish around, it takes only a day or two of observation to pattern when and where trout are feeding and to tailor your micronymphing to productive times and places.

For example, I often bracket tailwater hatches by micronymphing with an appropriate imitation. If I'm anticipating a hatch of *Baetis* mayflies between noon and 3 P.M., I head for good *Baetis* water by late morning, when nymphs are becoming active, and I micronymph just above the bottom or weed beds with a Chocolate Emerger. During the peak of a hatch, when trout are rising steadily, I usually switch to a dun imitation, but as a hatch tapers off, I revert to micronymphing and may continue to hook fish at a steady clip for more than an hour after other anglers have abandoned a hatch.

So far I've stressed the importance of micronymphing with a drag-free drift, but there are few absolutes in fishing, and I've had great action on tailwaters by actively stripping a small nymph, especially through big back eddies. Tailwater trout that specialize in feeding in slow eddies often resemble lake fish in their feeding tactics. They tend to cruise for their food, and moving prey grabs their attention. When fishing eddies, I remove the indicator so that I can sink my micronymph to any depth, and I cast right to visible fish and watch how they respond. Through trial and observation, I can often fine-tune my retrieve to trigger strikes.

Tailwater trout often establish feeding stations in the channels between weed beds. Channels with clean sand bottoms seem particularly attractive to trout, probably because a light-colored bottom serves as a high-contrast backdrop to highlight the tiny organisms that wash out of weeds. When I spot a fish in a weed channel, I stalk it from behind and use a reach cast to drop a dark micronymph a few feet above it, and then let the current roll the nymph along the clean bottom right to the fish. I remove the indicator and watch the fish. If it shifts laterally or tips down, I strike. Some channels have several good trout lined up single file, and you can pick them off in succession.

The more I micronymph, the more variations I find for fooling difficult trout. That's the beauty of micronymphing—it's a subtle technique that can save the day on trout that are lethargic, spooked, or just well educated. And it plays equally well on famous tailwaters or local creeks.

Chapter 5

Streamer Tactics

More than any other category of flies, streamers are designed for prospecting. They're big enough—and sometimes loud or flashy enough—to be readily spotted by trout, and they can be worked actively to cover a lot of water. Streamers have another very endearing quality: They annoy big fish. Imitating aquatic insects is the foundation of fly fishing, but in many waters, top-end trout specialize in bushwhacking the large, meaty food forms that streamers mimic. When you do tie into a real tackle buster, you hope it's on a streamer, because your odds of beaching it increase directly in proportion to the size of your hook and tippet.

RIVER TACTICS
I always look forward to heading west, because the freestone rivers of the Rockies are tailor-made for conventional streamer tactics that I don't get to employ much on small midwestern streams. Rivers have spacious runs where you can achieve long, enticing swings and drifts, plus the backcasting room to let you operate. On rivers, it's also easy to stay hidden from trout while casting across current, and presenting the fly broadside to the current lets you impart seductive, lifelike action while you control the speed of the drift.

Tailor your presentation to the mode that trout are in. If they're active and on scattered feeding stations, then cover lots of water quickly, just as you would in long-line nymphing. Keep most of your presentations in a horizontal plane with line, leader, and fly outstretched (even on big rivers, sinking the fly just a few feet is sufficient to cover most feeding stations). Cover nearby water first, and then lengthen your casts until you've covered feeding lies along the far bank. After covering each promising lie, I move upstream to a new casting position.

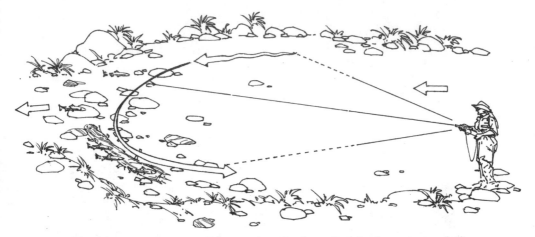

Down-and-Across Streamer Presentation. At the end of the downstream drift, the streamer swings back across the current on a fixed length of line, allowing an angler to methodically probe rocky pocket water or to cover the upstream face of a snag.

When active trout are holding fairly shallow, I usually present a streamer across current. That shows the fly to the trout broadside, and most streamers have a much bolder profile when viewed from the side rather than head-on. A streamer that's broadside to current also flutters and flashes more seductively. By casting across current and fishing the fly through a downstream swing, you keep the fly at the point of the presentation so it reaches feeding stations ahead of the line and leader. And by fishing across or down, you keep the fly on a tight line so that trout literally hook themselves.

In streamer fishing, there's often no visible sign of a strike; the jolt is the first indication. But observe the zone around the fly intently, because if you can spot the flash or form of a launching fish, you'll be prepared for a sudden strike. There's another incentive to keep your eyes peeled: Streamers are terrific "locator" flies that move some dandy trout that don't wind up striking. If you can spot a big fish as it moves to inspect your streamer, you might take it with a different presentation or at a time when it's feeding more aggressively.

In conventional across-and-down streamer fishing, a sinking-tip line allows you to sink unweighted streamers, which flutter and move enticingly. A moderately fast sinking tip of just 10 to 13 feet presents an unweighted streamer deep enough to cover most feeding stations, even in fast water. A short leader of 3 to 5 feet keeps the fly down at the level of the sinking tip.

Actively pumping or stripping a streamer enhances the impression of a dying or injured baitfish. Always pump and probe around boulders that are big enough to deflect current; just in front of and behind rocks are slow cushions where fish can hold with ease in fast water as they watch for passing prey to ambush. As a streamer reaches the downstream end of its drift and begins to swing back across current on a tight line, you can probe around boulders and deadfalls in numerous current lanes as you march the fly back to your side of the river.

A lot of strikes come as the fly reaches the end of the swing and hangs straight downstream from your position. Rather than pick the fly up abruptly, dart it upstream for a few yards to create the impression that the fly is panicking or attempting to escape. That often triggers a strike from an indecisive trout that has followed the fly for some distance.

When big-river trout are inactive and holding in deep refuge water, streamer fishing becomes a vertical game. Casting your fly upstream and fishing it on a dead drift gets it deeper than fishing it on a swing. Fishing a streamer dead drift isn't much different than high-stick nymphing, and it calls for similar rigging and line control. I usually rig with a floating line and a weighted streamer, and I add split shot to the tippet as needed to keep the fly in the productive bottom zone. A strike indicator high on the leader butt telegraphs takes. For dead-drift streamer fishing, I like a bulky fly tied with soft materials that cuts a strong silhouette when viewed from any angle and that pulsates enticingly, even when I'm not imparting action.

SMALL-STREAM TACTICS

Fishing streamers on narrow creeks requires creative presentations. Often you can't cast across current without looming right over the fish, so most casts must be made upstream or down at fairly sharp angles.

For upstream presentations to active fish, I use the same rigging and approach that I use for long-line nymphing. I stay well back from a run and fire relatively long casts that cover one or two specific feeding stations. Small streamers, in sizes 8 to 12, are easy to deliver on target with light-line rods. For upstream dead-drift presentations, I like soft streamers that pulsate with the current.

On small streams, good fish routinely seek overhead cover under snags, deadfalls, and bridges. If an obstruction spans the stream channel, the only viable presentation is usually downstream. By casting down and across to the far bank, you can dance a streamer back across the face of an obstruction on a fixed line. Use a tippet of 3X or stronger, because a big trout only has to bolt a short distance to reach serious cover, and unless you can keep it on a short leash, it's gone. Tippet diameter has minimal effect on a tight-line presentation anyway, so you might as well beef it up.

On a narrow creek, you can often approach a snag or deadfall from below and dap a streamer across its upstream face. As long as you stay slightly behind the obstruction, trout that are lurking beneath it can't see you. With a quiet approach, they'll never know you're there. If you hook a powerful fish while dapping under a snag, immediately move upstream to gain leverage and improve your fighting angle.

A fly with a weighted head can be dapped or jigged with an erratic up-and-down action. It also sinks a couple feet when it's hanging downstream in current on a fixed line, which allows you to probe under snags. For dapping and downstream presentations, I tie some streamers with metal dumbbell eyes, but any streamer can be made front-heavy by sliding a big split shot tight to the hook eye. Incidentally, streamers with weighted heads are also the ticket for casting upstream into very fast chutes, because they plummet quickly and ride in the productive bottom zone throughout the drift.

Even small streams allow some cross-current streamer presentations. When I encounter an exceptionally big pool, I usually kneel and fish from the shallow inside bank so that I can cast across current and impart action to the fly as I probe along the deep outer bank.

As you work your way up a brushy creek, be alert to the built-in advantages you hold on a dogleg run (that's where fast water piles against a vertical bank and deflects at a right angle). Where current piles against the bank, it usually scours a depression or undercuts the bank, creating a choice feeding lie. As you fish upstream into a dogleg, simply cast to the far side of the fast entry chute and let the current sweep your streamer broadside through the deep depression along the outside bank. Essentially, a dogleg allows for a cross-current streamer presentation, yet you're facing straight upstream so you can use the stream channel for unobstructed backcasting space. On the small, brushy creeks that most fly fishers avoid, doglegs are among the most productive runs and the easiest to fish.

LAKE TACTICS

In a river, the bottom of an exceptionally deep pool might be a couple degrees cooler than the surface, but in a lake, the water 10 or 20 feet down can easily be 5 to 10 degrees cooler than the top. Consequently, trout in lakes shift vertically to stay in comfortable temperature zones. On sizzling summer days when stream trout are lethargic, lake fish often continue to feed actively in the cool depths. That's especially true on lakes where the water stratifies into definite temperature bands.

The key to cracking lakes is locating active fish. That's easier said than done, because you're dealing with a lot of water, and most of it is empty. That's where streamers really shine. They're big and flashy enough to be readily seen by trout in dimly lit depths, and they can be fished much faster than nymphs or wet flies, so you can prospect a lot of water quickly.

For fishing down to 15 feet, a 13-foot sinking-tip line is sufficient. For fishing much deeper, full-sinking lines are needed. A fast-sinking line gets your streamer down quickly, but once it reaches the desired level, it takes a steady retrieve to keep it there. Slow-sinking lines take longer to drop, but then they keep your fly at a constant depth, even on a slow retrieve.

Most of the lakes that I fish in the high Rockies or on the Canadian Shield are weed-free, and my favorite tactic is to lay a full-sinking line right on the bottom and use a buoyant streamer that rises off the bottom. Many streamer patterns can be tied with buoyant underbodies of closed-cell foam, but my ace is a realistic mylar minnow imitation that I call the Bobbing Baitfish. I retrieve the fly with long, arm-length strips, pausing several seconds between strips. When I strip the fly, it dives to follow the path of the sinking line. Between strips, the fly rises several feet; the length of the leader and the duration of the pause are the limiting factors. It's a very erratic wounded-minnow action that really triggers strikes. Since a buoyant fly rises off the bottom between strips rather than dropping into the rocks, like a weighted fly, it's also a remarkably snag-proof tactic that lets me work the productive bottom zone without hanging constantly. I often strip the fly until I feel it touch the bottom, and then let it rise. If the fly hangs on the bottom, I simply roll-cast excess line beyond the fly so that I can exert a reverse pull to buoy it off the rocks. At times, I also prospect with the Bobbing Baitfish at midlevels for suspended fish. I've yet to find a predatory game fish that won't whack it. In addition to accounting for a lot of trout, the Bobbing Baitfish is easily my best walleye fly on lakes, and it produces many of my heaviest smallmouth bass and northern pike.

On lakes, it's easy to keep a streamer in the productive bottom zone by casting from shore and retrieving up the incline. When you retrieve away from shore, you're pulling the fly up and away from the bottom with each strip, so you need a slow retrieve or a heavily weighted fly to stay near the bottom. If you're casting from watercraft, you can position yourself to cast parallel to shore and retrieve along the bottom at a constant depth. That's a great tactic if you've determined that fish are active at a specific depth or are cruising weed lines or dropoffs.

Most fly fishers have forsaken canoes for float tubes, kickboats, and kayaks, which certainly have their uses, but I still do much of my lake fishing from a canoe. Sitting in a canoe seat with a backrest is infinitely more comfortable than dangling from a float tube or sitting flat in a kayak. In a canoe, you sit higher, so you have better casting and hooking leverage and an improved angle for seeing below the surface to spot fish or structure. When it comes to exploring big water, float tubes and kickboats are just too immobile. Kayaks can cover water and carry enough gear for camping, but they're tedious to load, which makes them impractical for portaging. A canoe has a yoke for portaging and an open hull to hold big gear packs, and a decent solo paddler can cover upward of 20 miles a day.

Granted, in a tube or kickboat, you can use your feet to control your position as you cast, but you can learn to control a canoe even when fishing solo. To hold stationary in wind, I use a mesh anchor bag that holds the rock of my choice (a rock of about 8 pounds anchors a canoe in a moderate breeze). I anchor only in shallow to moderate depths, so 30 feet of 1/4-inch polypropylene boat rope is sufficient. To keep the anchor positioned off the front of the canoe, thread the rope under the front carry handle. (If your canoe lacks built-in handles, a small loop of rope can act as a guide.) Knot the free end of the anchor rope to the center thwart. When moving, suspend the anchor from the front of the canoe, and secure the rope around the base of a yoke pad. With a little experimentation, you'll learn to rig the anchor bag so that it hangs entirely above the waterline. Dropping anchor is a simple one-handed operation—just pay out rope until the anchor hits bottom, and then lock the rope around a yoke pad with a couple quick turns.

In June, I usually make a solo canoe trip primarily to fly-fish for big smallmouth bass in Ontario, but many of the same waters also hold lake trout. By early summer, lakers are already feeding 20 to 40 feet down, and they can be much deeper if the weather is unseasonably hot. That's definitely full-sinking-line territory, and the trout are widely scattered over intimidating, wind-swept expanses. Often I just let the canoe drift with the wind while I trail an entire sinking fly line, plus some backing. Keeping the canoe at a right angle to the waves is safer than drifting broadside, and it slows the drift to a more productive pace. To control a canoe one-handed while holding a rod, grab a paddle just above the blade and tuck the handle under your back—you'll have enough leverage to hold a straight line or make turns. For deep-water lake trout, I usually run a streamer that has a strong profile and plenty of flash, such as a Deceiver. Lake trout respond well to a jigging action, so I slide a couple big split-shot against the hook eye and pump the fly to make it rise and fall erratically. Big-water trout and salmon that feed at considerable depths primarily hunt cold-water forage fish such as ciscoes, alewives, smelt, and herring, which also range deep in search of comfortable temperatures. All of these baitfish are basically silver in color, so light-colored streamers with silver flash are usually workable imitations.

Actively trolling a streamer from a canoe lets you quickly prospect water on a controlled course, so it's a great way to contact trout on low-density lakes. You can always switch to a more deliberate technique once you're into fish. For trolling deeper than 20 feet, you need a fly line with an extremely fast sink rate, because fly lines have enough diameter that they plane when trolled and run higher than you'd expect. When you're trolling shallow, say 8 to 15 feet deep, that tendency to plane becomes an advantage, because you can pay out an entire moderately fast-sinking fly line plus some backing to run the fly well behind any backwash created by the canoe, and yet you'll rarely hang on the bottom. When trolling a streamer, I achieve hands-free hook sets by wedging the fly reel between a thigh and a canoe seat, to lock the spool, and then bracing the lower rod shaft against my opposite shin. I use the paddle to impart action to the streamer. I paddle on the side of the canoe opposite the rod, and I start each stroke with a roundhouse sweep to throw the nose of the canoe toward the rod and put slack into the line. At the end of the stroke, I pry off the gunwale to throw the nose of the canoe in the opposite direction and move the fly on a tight line; that's when most strikes are detected.

Sinking lines tend to sag in the water, so you have to move some line for solid hook sets. When retrieving, keep the rod tip low and pointed at the line; move the fly by stripping the line rather than pumping the rod tip. From a sitting position, you have reduced hooking leverage, so it's especially critical to keep the rod tip down. As you set the hook, haul down on the line with your stripping hand while you raise the rod sharply. Rather than sweeping back with the rod tip, raise the entire rod shaft so that the butt section helps drive a big streamer hook through bone or cartilage.

A few lake situations call for unweighted streamers and floating lines. When baitfish are breaking the surface, a trout may be chasing them very close to the top. At night, a floating line and a buoyant streamer create a surface commotion that trout home in on.

Other lake situations call for fishing a weighted streamer on a floating line, although it's rarely practical to attempt to fish much deeper than the length of your leader. With a floating line and a weighted fly, you can hop the fly along the bottom and even kick up silt to simulate a crayfish or a darting sculpin. When sight-casting to trout that are cruising subsurface, a weighted fly drops quickly to their level, yet you can easily pick a floating line off the water for multiple presentations before a fish moves out of range.

With so many types of fly lines available, plus an array of synthetic tying materials that have opened up streamer design, there are really no limits to the lake depths you can plumb or the actions you can achieve with streamers. They're simply great prospecting flies that are fascinating to experiment with.

Chapter 6

Prospecting
with Dry Flies

Between hatches, I prospect with nymphs and streamers most of the time, because when trout aren't rising to naturals, sinking an imitation to the level of the fish is usually more productive than skimming the surface. And on many waters, top-end trout are rarely caught on drys, even during blizzard hatches.

But at times, prospecting with a dry fly can yield fast action and stout trout. When conditions are favorable, I prefer to search with a dry, because surface strikes are exciting and casting a dry is so enjoyable. Let's look at favorable situations for prospecting on top.

TEMPERATURE

Sluggish trout that have retired to refuge lies rarely rocket off the bottom to inhale drys. The best time to prospect with a dry is when trout are dispersed to feeding stations (on moving water) or are actively cruising for food (in stillwater). That generally happens when water temperatures are in the fifties or low sixties.

PACING

I only prospect with drys when trout are aggressive, and aggressive trout usually strike on the first presentation. So when I prospect with drys, I move right along, covering new water with each cast. The more fish I can show the fly to while they remain aggressive, the more strikes I'll generate. When I bump into a concentration of fish, I gear down and work more thoroughly until strikes taper off. Then I get moving again. Whether I'm fishing small streams or big rivers, I often prospect 3 to 5 miles of water in a day.

POPULATION PROFILE

I always consider the makeup of a fish population when deciding whether or not to prospect with a dry. If a stream is stuffed with pan-size trout that are in an aggressive mode, I go right to a dry and have a riot. But if a stream harbors nice browns that specialize in bushwhacking minnows and crayfish, I usually probe deep with a nymph or streamer, because prospecting with a dry all but nixes my chances of tangling with a trophy. On exceptionally fertile spring creeks and tailwaters, big trout often continue to forage heavily on small insects at the surface so they remain relatively susceptible to drys.

Regardless of water type, prospecting success with drys usually decreases as fishing pressure increases. Trout that are repeatedly caught and released become wary of what they ingest and aren't likely to rise freely unless worthwhile numbers of naturals are on the surface.

Cutthroat and brook trout thrive mainly in pristine areas where fishing pressure is light and summer water temperatures are cool, so I routinely prospect on top for these species.

STREAM TYPES

High-gradient freestone streams of moderate fertility are tailor-made for prospecting with attractor dry flies. Trout that inhabit such streams are rarely selective. They can't afford to pass up many meals, and they must capture food quickly before it's swept away. The Rockies have many examples of this water type. Some heavily fished freestone rivers, such as the Gallatin and the lower Madison, fish reasonably well with attractor drys between hatches. But the best rivers for prospecting with drys are in the backcountry, where trout see few anglers. On rivers like the South Fork of the Flathead, deep in Montana's Bob Marshall Wilderness, cutthroat trout still rise boldly to attractors. The fishing is very simple and immensely relaxing, and you can easily lose yourself in the rhythms of casting and the solitude of the river.

As streams lose gradient and increase in fertility, prospecting with a dry becomes more demanding. Trout get a better look at the fly, so imitations must look natural and convincing. When there's abundant food in the drift, trout won't move far to intercept a fly. On the plus side, when trout density is high, you can show the fly to a lot of fish in a short span, and you can often identify specific zones, such as back eddies or riffle margins, where trout are particularly susceptible to drys.

Two streams can have identical trout densities, fertility, and forage bases, but they may fish very differently depending on the configuration of their channels and how fish are distributed. If trout are clustered into a few big pools with long expanses of dead water in between, prospecting with a dry won't be highly productive, even if you manage to pick off a few fish in each good pool. But if trout are evenly distributed in a good mix of runs, riffles, and pocket water, you can cover good lies at a steady clip and constantly show the fly to fresh fish.

EARLY-SEASON PROSPECTING

By late spring, water temperatures hover near optimal for much of the day, and trout see frequent mayfly and caddis hatches. Since fish are active and conditioned to looking up, it's prime time to prospect on top.

On big freestone rivers, go right to a substantial dry fly, like a Wulff in size 12 or 14. A heavily hackled fly cuts a bold silhouette that's easily spotted by trout at a distance, and it floats high, so you can see it. Attractor drys, like Wulffs and Humpies, are often tied in loud colors, but I tie most of mine in natural shades so that I can also use them to match hatches of big mayflies, like green drakes.

In spring, before terrestrials become abundant, an adult caddis is usually my prospecting dry of choice. Caddis simply have many good attributes for searching the surface. They're more abundant than mayflies on most waters, and adult caddis commonly survive for a couple weeks, so trout get used to seeing them daily and taking them opportunistically. There's really no unnatural way to fish an adult caddis imitation—it can be dead drifted, skated, or pulled subsurface to imitate a diving egg layer. The down-wing caddis profile suggests many other common insects, including large midges, immature grasshoppers, and small stoneflies. Palmered hairwing patterns, like the Elk Hair Caddis, are buoyant and easy to see on the water, and very durable.

TERRESTRIAL TIME

Terrestrials abound along most trout water. From early summer right into autumn, their imitations are consistently among the top drys for prospecting. Few anglers appreciate just how frequently land-based insects wind up in the drink, but that point was driven home to me many years ago when I cleaned a foot-long brown trout for a shore lunch and discovered thirteen hoppers in its gullet. And it was still before noon! Imagine how many hoppers that trout might have ingested once the afternoon warmth and wind really stirred the insects into action.

Wind knocks flying insects onto the water and shakes crawling insects from streamside vegetation. Whenever wind gusts trigger an increase in the rising tempo of trout, be quick to suspect terrestrials as the main course. Likewise, summer downpours flush a smorgasbord of terrestrials into streams.

Ants

Ants seemingly thrive everywhere, from damp woodlands to lush meadows to arid grasslands, and trout relish them. A convincing ant imitation is one of the best bets for fooling sophisticated spring-creek trout between hatches. The drawback to prospecting with an ant is that it's a relatively small terrestrial that's not visible to trout at a distance and doesn't hit the water with an audible splat, as a big terrestrial does. Rather than prospecting blindly with ants, I usually reserve them for precise presentations to located fish. Ant imitations are easier to track on the water if you add wings to your patterns. In summer, I always tote winged imitations, because flying ants can collect on the water in droves, and I've seen trout reject flies that weren't kissing cousins to the naturals right down to size, color, and wing configuration.

Beetles

Beetles occur in a staggering array of sizes and colors, but for prospecting, a standard black beetle in size 14 usually turns the trick. It's plump enough to make a fish-attracting splat as it hits flat water, and that splat can trigger a strike if the fly lands behind a fish or outside of its normal feeding lane. Even if you can't see a beetle once its on the water, being able to see its impact point tells you whether your cast was on the money and has you watching the right zone for a take. You can boost the visibility of beetle patterns by dabbing fluorescent paint on their backs or by adding wings or a post of bright yarn.

I often prospect with a beetle in early summer before flying hoppers abound. In late summer, I prospect with a beetle mostly in the evening after hopper activity has subsided for the day. When trout are bunched, a beetle is usually my terrestrial of choice, because it can be fished more subtly than a large hopper and often triggers multiple strikes from a pod of fish.

Crickets

Crickets abound in meadows that hold lots of hoppers, but they also thrive in damp, shaded woodlands where hoppers are scarce (a plump cricket imitation is my favorite prospecting dry for woodland brook trout). Unlike hoppers, crickets are active in the low light and cool temperatures of dusk and dawn, and on rainy days. A black cricket cuts a bold silhouette against a dark or overcast sky, and I often pump the fly to create a disturbance that trout home in on. If you haven't been fishing cricket, that's the niche to start with—by working them aggressively, with splats and movement in low light.

Grasshoppers

I always look forward to grasshopper time, especially the banner years, when waves of hoppers flush at every step and rattle like hailstones in the parched grasses. Meadows hold the most naturals and are the prime areas to work. Populations of mature, winged hoppers peak in August and September. Hoppers are activated by dry wind and warmth, so hopper fishing is usually best from late morning into early evening. Of course, you still have to find active fish, so in hot weather, head for waters that remain cool. In the Midwest, I often target the meadow sections of small headwater tributaries. By late summer, little meadow streams tunnel under overhanging grass, but trout are there in the cool water and ready to pounce.

Fortunately for anglers, grasshoppers fly just well enough that they frequently crash land on water. Most hoppers tumble in along stream edges, and those that alight in midstream usually kick toward shore. Cutbanks and overhanging grass are attractive ambush points that provide trout with midday shade and overhead protection from predators. On overgrown streams, I frequently cast a hopper into weeds (intentionally or otherwise) and then pull it onto the water. To free a fly that's draped over a weed, limb, or fence strand, don't just jerk and hope. Slowly draw slack out of the line as you raise the fly to within inches of the obstruction, and then give a quick flip of the wrist—the fly should vault cleanly over the obstruction.

Natural hoppers hit the middle of small streams with some regularity, so it can pay to fire a cast to the center of a run before moving on. But on broad rivers, hopper-seeking trout patrol the banks almost exclusively, because that's the only zone where naturals are frequently encountered. It's enlightening to present hoppers to visible trout on big rivers and watch how they respond. Trout that are stationed within a few feet of a bank will strike or take a very serious look at a well-presented hopper nearly every time. Trout that are just 5 to 10 yards from shore will show interest in a hopper only about half the time. Trout that are stationed in midriver are highly unlikely to move for a hopper. I've seen this scenario repeated so many times that when I fish a hopper on big rivers, I pound as many miles of bank as possible and pretty much ignore other water.

Trout tend to strike hoppers reflexively on the first presentation or not at all, so fire just a cast or two to each promising lie and move on. But don't charge ahead blindly—scan all shallows, including water that looks too thin to hold a respectable fish, because big trout commonly ambush hoppers in less than a foot of water. Look for irregularities on the stream bottom—when trout are in thin water under a bright sun, a normally insignificant depression or rock can harbor a 4-pound fish. When wind is buffeting the water, it's especially easy to overlook a good fish that's sitting wide open in the shallows. Incidentally, it's a myth that bright sun makes it uncomfortable for trout to hold in shallow water. When it's bright, their eyes adjust to admit less light. Provided that water temperatures are comfortable, big trout don't hesitate to prowl sun-drenched shallows at hopper time.

Anytime you can spot a trout before you present a hopper in its zone for the first time, your chances for a hookup jump dramatically. On a big river a good approach is to wade with the sun at your back and cast toward the bank (pick the bank that's most conducive to that approach in the afternoon). Putting the sun at your back greatly reduces glare so you can see bottom details and fish. Casting toward the bank also gives you unlimited backcasting room and makes it easy to avoid lining fish, since you're dropping just the fly—and not the line—in the productive bank zone.

When a trout is visible, I like to drop a hopper on the upstream edge of its window of vision. A fish that actually hears or sees a hopper touch down will often charge the fly and grab it without careful inspection. If a trout elects to study the fly as it floats downstream, a drag-free drift is usually critical to eliciting a strike. Maintain a natural drift as long as possible, because an indecisive trout may well turn and follow a hopper downstream as it carefully eyeballs the fly. Watching a hefty brown follow, study, and eventually inhale a hopper is always riveting. It's an advantage to be able to see a trailing fish and to realize exactly what's happening, because when that snout finally breaks the surface, you must delay the strike or you'll snatch the fly away. As soon as a trailing fish inhales your fly, it will turn back upstream toward its established feeding station. Strike just as the fish makes that turn. Big trout often take hoppers and other drys more deliberately than small trout do, so when you see a big snout, slow down your hook set—if you can.

On slow slicks, I slap a hopper on the surface, because the noise of the impact radiates much farther than on moving water. Slapping the fly onto flat water can spark an explosive charge by a trout that's 20 feet away—and that's an exciting strike to witness. On slack water, I let the fly sit stationary for just a few seconds after impact. Then I pump it to create a lifelike disturbance and to move the fly within range of trout that didn't detect the impact. On steadily moving water, I rarely pump a hopper, because the current transports the fly within view of waiting fish anyway, and drawing the slack out of the line and leader to move the fly works against a drag-free float for the balance of the drift.

On rivers that hold rainbows and browns, the percentage of big, healthy browns in my catch usually soars when hopper fishing is hot. Foraging browns are bank huggers by nature, and they prefer substantial prey, so it's not surprising that they often specialize in hunting hoppers. One September afternoon on the Green River below Flaming Gorge in Utah, I ran better than twenty consecutive browns on hoppers at a time when the river was producing a preponderance of rainbows. On Wisconsin streams, I catch some of my largest dry-fly browns of the year on hoppers. There just aren't many times when you can prospect with a dry and have a legitimate shot at dominant fish—that's what makes hopper time so exciting!

BACK EDDIES AND SCUM SUCKERS

Large rivers typically have big back eddies. Most eddies are on the outer margins of pools, where current deflects against banks and slowly curls back on itself in an upstream direction. All sorts of flotsam collects in eddies, from nymphal shucks to drowned emergers to spentwings. Even in winter and late summer, when caddis and mayfly hatches are uncommon, midges regularly hover around slow water. Eddies accumulate their heaviest payloads after hatches, spinner falls, or other spikes in insect activity, so it's not unusual to find pods of rising fish in quiet backwaters when snouts aren't showing anywhere else on a river. An increase in river level to boost power generation flushes banks, pockets, and side channels, also causing a buildup of food in eddies. Some scum lines are so dense that they look like oil slicks when viewed from a low angle or in flat light.

On many of the best tailwaters, a sort of underclass of the trout population specializes in feeding in slack water. Compared to their current-loving brethren, eddy trout have distinctively different feeding habits. Most notably, when eddy trout are feeding on the surface, they actively cruise for their food, just as lake fish do. I refer to eddy trout as an underclass because they typically have skinny physiques compared with current-dwelling trout from the same fishery, due to several factors. Dominant trout are highly protective of their feeding stations, so on rivers with high-fish densities, a lot of subordinate fish are driven off the prime moving-water stations and wind up scavenging the slack water in loose packs. While a given eddy may collect a steady stream of food, it can also have two dozen adult trout competing for forage in an area the size of a back-yard swimming pool, so individual fish aren't ingesting huge quantities. Also, since eddy fish must actively cruise for much of their food, net energy gain is marginal, and fish don't pack on excess weight. That

Most eddy trout cruise and sip from the scum which collects in the eddy whorl. Typically, a few trout also feed from fixed stations along the slow, shallow inside bank (often in a narrow channel between the bank and weedbeds). Note that although these bank-side trout are facing into the current, they're oriented downstream.

doesn't mean eddy fish aren't worth pursuing, because in catch-and-release tailwaters, where most trout survive for several years, eddy fish can still average 14 to 17 inches and 1 to 2 pounds. But you'll rarely see a real brute cruising and sipping the eddies.

Since eddy fish are nutritionally challenged, they prowl almost continually, and that's worth remembering when you're looking for surface action during slow periods. Stout, healthy trout chow down when water temperatures are favorable or food is readily available, but stressed trout often continue to prowl when temperatures are marginal and pickings are slim. That's a point I've had driven home to me time and again in my many years of fishing high-altitude lakes in the Rockies. On lakes that are overpopulated with skinny fish, the action is usually nonstop. On lakes that support a low density of trophy fish, feeding is usually compressed into short intervals when conditions are favorable. Incidentally, on rivers that hold a mix of rainbows and browns, most eddy fish are bows. That's a reflection of the rainbows' preference for smaller food forms and the more aggressive nature of browns.

In eddy fishing, you get a lot of nose-to-fly inspections and maddening last-instant refusals. The natural response of most anglers is to switch flies constantly, as they scramble to find the magic bullet. But since eddies collect a smorgasbord of flotsam, selectivity is rarely the issue. What you're up against in tailwater eddies are trout that get a close, undistorted look at your fly and that are simply masters at detecting phonies, since they see so many. Also, while eddy water may look stationary, it's still deflecting in nearly invisible currents that create subtle drag. That's why I usually stick with a size 20 or smaller midge imitation (either an adult or an emerger) fished right in the surface film. Small flies have fewer glaring artificialities than big flies, and they can be presented on fine tippets to combat subtle drag (2 to 3 feet of 6X tippet is standard rigging for eddies). Rather than throwing everything in your box, the key to success often lies in targeting a specific fish by repeatedly dropping your fly in its path until you achieve a perfectly natural presentation. I routinely catch eddy fish on the same fly that they've already eyeballed and refused several times.

Since eddy fish cruise between rises, you have to observe their rising intervals and deliver the fly on rhythm where they're likely to rise next. It's easier to stay right on a trout's path through a series of presentations if you cast from an elevated position that allows you to see a fish while it's cruising subsurface between rises. On some of the canyon tailwaters where I target eddy fish, I cast from the tops of big boulders. In this situation, I don't worry about fish seeing me. Tailwater trout are so used to seeing a steady parade of anglers that they aren't about to alter their behavior unless you start throwing rocks or try to ride them. Hey, if it wasn't possible to catch trout that can read the logo on your waders, then shuffling wouldn't be such a deadly technique that it's been banned on most tailwaters.

Eddy trout often cruise established routes, just like lake fish do. These routes are usually circular, and on a big eddy, they can approach 100 feet in diameter. At regular intervals, a given fish will pass into easy range and then fade into marginal range. Casting 80 or 90 feet across several conflicting current seams is not the way to hook these trout consistently. You want to lock onto a specific fish while it's close and pepper its path with a series of casts. As that fish moves away, switch to a new target. By working from a lofty position, you can usually track several cruisers simultaneously and pound the fish that's on the most favorable route.

When food is scattered, eddy trout cruise big routes and cover some water between rises. When food is abundant, they wallow in tight little circles and rise almost constantly. When a major eddy is really on, you can have two dozen fish grazing within easy range. Most tailwaters provide steady eddy action throughout the day, but often the water really boils in late evening after the nine-to-five crowd has bolted for cocktails and T-bones. It's always satisfying to end the day with a flurry of strikes and to know you've really milked it. For that kind of memorable action, I'll gladly hike out alone by flashlight and eat a late dinner out of a can.

PROSPECTING LAKES

On lakes, I prospect subsurface most of the time, especially on trophy fisheries, because big trout tend to feed deep, and sinking the fly to their level is usually more productive than trying to force them up. But when the surface of a lake goes glassy, I often prospect with a dry by skating the fly to create a wake that cruising trout can detect from a distance (flies with stiff, palmered hackle have superior skating properties). Much of my lake fishing is at high altitude, where calm conditions occur mainly in evening as the sinking sun stops fueling rising thermals. After probing deep all day, it's a welcome change of pace to switch to a dry and work the top when the wind drops. Since trout can easily detect insects on a flat surface, they rise more willingly when winds are light.

At times, wind becomes a dry-fly fisher's ally by blowing assorted insects into concentrated scum lines that collect along lee shores. When wind is driving insects landward, trout will work within feet of shore. On windy afternoons, I often walk leeward shores and check for this type of action. Binoculars are handy for spotting distant pockets of rising fish.

Whether I'm prospecting with a dry or matching a hatch, on lakes I get more surface strikes by casting into the wind than with it, and here's why. When I strip the fly to attract the attention of fish, I'm removing slack from the line. When I'm not stripping the fly, it can only drift naturally if it's blowing toward me. If the fly is hanging downwind on a tight line, it's being restrained unnaturally and can even be pulled under the surface.

It's funny how easily overlooked factors can make a difference, but I often notice that it's much easier to take fish that are stationed to a particular side of me. The reasons vary. Perhaps a stiff crosswind is aiding reach casts to my left but killing casts to my right. Perhaps fish that are stationed to my left are picking up rod glare or casting shadows that fish to my right aren't. In poor light, trout may be able to readily see flies that are silhouetted against the open sky but not against bankside foliage. Always be on the lookout for patterns in strikes or refusals, because if you can pick up on a pattern, you can target the most susceptible fish and ride a hot streak while conditions hold.

Chapter 7

Some Top Prospecting Flies and What Makes Them Tick

This chapter is not a comprehensive listing of the best prospecting flies; rather, it discusses the design elements that make certain flies winners. The patterns that are discussed have earned reserved parking spaces in my fly boxes, and if you toted nothing else, you'd be well equipped to prospect most trout water. But there are many other excellent patterns, with new ones being created all the time, and whether you buy or tie your flies, you're ahead of the game if you can recognize potent prospecting flies for various situations.

Having confidence in your fly is never more critical than when you're prospecting. When you lack confidence, you become inattentive and sloppy. But when you have faith that your fly will move trout if you fish it well enough, then you remain focused and your results usually reflect it. So make a sound fly choice based on conditions, and then give that fly a legitimate shot.

If you aren't a fly tier, you should seriously consider taking the plunge, because in the long run it will make you a better angler. Tying forces you to look closely at natural organisms and critically at fly design. By tying, you control every variable of the flies you fish, including profile, materials, weighting, color, size, and hook style, and that gives you the versatility to solve many of the riddles you encounter on the water.

If you already tie but would like to boost the variety and effectiveness of your prospecting flies, the surest route is to experiment with lots of different tying materials and to observe their properties. That naturally leads to innovation, as you recognize new uses for various materials. Being an innovative tier doesn't necessarily mean conjuring up entirely new patterns. Many of my top prospecting flies are variations on established patterns, and I've simply substituted superior materials or better tying technique to produce flies that fish to their full potential. An often over-looked advantage of designing your own flies is that on hard-fished waters, you can show trout new wrinkles rather than the standard imitations they're conditioned to reject. Consistently catching difficult trout on flies you've designed, and not just copied, takes fly fishing to a new level.

NYMPHS

Long-line nymphing is my single most productive prospecting method, and I usually sling a fuzzy, impressionistic nymph that moves naturally on a dead drift and offers opportunistic trout a substantial mouthful. Anatomically correct, hard-bodied nymphs look great sitting on coffee tables, but in the water, they lack translucency and motion. By comparison, fuzzy nymphs look buggy and alive. Their protruding fibers simulate working legs and gill filaments. And fuzzy nymphs diffuse light through their soft margins to simulate the translucency of living nymphs.

Trout can expel artificial nymphs so quickly that many pickups go undetected by anglers, but fish tend to hold soft imitations a bit longer, perhaps because they feel more natural than hard imitations. Some anglers have speculated that fuzzy nymphs catch on the vomerine teeth of trout and are actually more difficult to expel. Whatever the reason, there's no denying that roughed-up nymphs catch trout. It's a universal experience in nymphing—you start out with a neatly tied nymph, only to discover that the fly becomes more effective as the trout shred it almost beyond recognition.

On most fuzzy nymphs, the composition of the dubbing, and how it's teased, is the key design element. If you don't already have a dubbing blender on your tying table, then beg, borrow, or steal one so that you can create the precise dubbing mixtures you need. For exceptionally spiky nymphs, add lots of guard hairs to the dubbing mix. To create dubbings that have exceptional sparkle and translucency, add synthetic fibers, but chop them very short so that they tease easily; the synthetic fibers in most commercial dubbings are so long that they lock around the tying thread and don't tease readily. Many commercial dubbings, especially natural ones, vary in color and texture from lot to lot, and you pay a couple bucks for a skimpy bag that runs out just when you really need it. With a blender, you can kick out copious amounts of dubbing with very controlled characteristics. And by shaving whole hides and chopping your own synthetics from bulk yarns, you can blend big batches for peanuts.

Speaking of teasing, the finest metal dubbing teasers on the market have round handles, which make them prone to rolling off tying tables and into waste bins. I'm not a fan of steel-barbed dubbing teasers—they're tedious to use and can damage thread, ribbing, hackle stems, and wing cases. Nylon dubbing brushes are infinitely faster, more effective, and more forgiving. Nylon bristles won't nick or sever delicate materials, so you can brush quickly and vigorously. From sweeping hackle to fuzzing wing cases, you can do some nifty things with a dubbing brush that you can't begin to do with a metal pick. Brushing is so versatile and effective that it has become an integral design element of many of my dubbed nymphs, streamers, and emergers.

I've never seen a suitable dubbing brush marketed as a fly-tying tool, but the gun-cleaning brush that I use is ideal. It's not a bore brush—it's designed for scrubbing gun parts. It's basically a toothbrush on one end with a handle that tapers to a single row of short, stiff nylon bristles on the opposite end (the business end). I chop the handle in half and discard the toothbrush portion. The short, stiff bristles have remarkable teasing power, while the single-row configuration can be applied with precision. I can quickly fuzz an entire dubbed body by raking it lengthwise, or I can tease just a portion of a fly by raking at a right angle to the hook shank. Gun shops can order the brush from Brownell's catalog, and I've seen it packaged by Kleen Bore. If you have a belt sander, you can transform a toothbrush into a dandy dubbing brush in a jiffy—simply grind it down to a single row of bristles, and then use a sharp scissors to chop the bristles to about 3/16 inch in length; longer bristles are too soft.

Fuzzy Hare's Ear

The Gold-Ribbed Hare's Ear has probably taken more trout than any other nymph, which is amazing, considering that most commercial Hare's Ears are poorly tied—they're much too neat, smooth, and round. You can tie a Fuzzy Hare's Ear that's superior for prospecting. Begin by maintaining a high count of spiky guard hairs in your dubbing. Instead of Hare's Mask, I use the back fur from winter cottontail rabbits—it's loaded with mature guard hairs that I mix with soft underfur and about 20 percent clear Antron for added translucency. Dub a firm, oversize thorax that covers the entire front half of the hook shank, and then attack the finished nymph with a dubbing brush by raking from under the thorax up toward the edges of the wing case. Brushing flattens the oversize thorax ball into a robust clinger-crawler mayfly nymph profile and projects plenty of soft and spiky dubbing from the sides of the nymph to simulate legs and gills. (To obtain similar hair legs, most tiers resort to the tedious process of twisting guard hairs into dubbing loops.) Rib the abdomen with oval tinsel; it compresses less dubbing than flat tinsel so that the abdomen can be lightly fuzzed with just a few brush strokes. I rib with DMC metallic embroidery thread, which is sold in craft and fabric stores.

Mature mayfly nymphs, the most active and vulnerable kind, have dark, swollen wing pads that are nicely imitated with quill slips cut from the secondary flight feathers of Canada goose wings. Goose quill sections have smooth undersides and nappy topsides that are textured something like corduroy. I fold the quill section to expose the nap, and then stroke the finished wing case with the dubbing brush to stand the nap on end for a ripe, swollen appearance. The nap also catches and holds tiny air bubbles, enhancing translucency. Since most mature mayfly nymphs range from dark olive to rusty brown, I primarily prospect with a Chocolate Hare's Ear rather than the standard gray version.

Soft-Hackle Woolly Worm

Legions of fly fishers swear allegiance to the Woolly Bugger streamer but disregard its nymph/wet-fly counterpart—the Woolly Worm. That's mystifying to me, because Woolly Worms and Buggers share the same extraordinary fish appeal, and I find more applications for Woolly Worms, especially the small sizes, which can be cast with precision and fished very subtly. In fact, for nearly two decades, the Soft-Hackle Woolly Worm has been my top all-around prospecting fly by a runaway margin.

The Woolly Worm has survived and flourished in my fly boxes because it's an impressionistic subsurface fly that cuts across broad categories. It generally suggests a scud, stonefly nymph, damsel nymph, hellgrammite, and a host of other aquatic organisms from beetle larvae to big clambering caddis larvae. Whether viewed broadside or straight on, a well-tied Woolly Worm cuts a strong profile and just looks buggy and alive. And the Woolly Worm has other great prospecting attributes. It can be dead drifted like a nymph, swung like a wet fly, or stripped like a streamer. The most popular color, black, maintains a bold silhouette in low light and in deep or discolored water—conditions that usually beg for an effective prospecting fly. The Woolly Worm can be tied big or small, and even the diminutive size 16 version seems to entice the kind of big, predatory trout that specialize in bushwhacking much larger prey. There are darned few prospecting flies that can walk that line—that are small and light enough to be fished far and fine, yet consistently move top-end fish.

The Woolly Worm has always ranked among my favorite prospecting flies, but as I advanced as a tier, I recognized that the materials used in the standard pattern are wanting. In particular, the rooster saddle hackle used on most ties is stiff and web-free—it doesn't pulsate seductively, and it vanishes in low light or cloudy water, greatly diminishing the bugginess of the fly.

The inspiration to rebuild the Woolly came a couple decades back, when I saw my first Metz hen neck. It had a combination of properties I'd never seen in a neck. The hackle was soft and webby, yet the feathers were long enough to palmer several turns over a chunky body. With the right hackle in hand, I knew I could build a better Woolly, but while I was at it, I overhauled the fly from scratch.

For the body, I scrap the standard chenille and go with soft rabbit, which I dub to form a natural forward taper and then brush for a super-buggy effect. Dubbing increases the time required to tie a Woolly, especially a big one, but I speed things up by building a foundation with Purr-fect Punch embroidery yarn and then dubbing a layer of fur over the foundation. Punch yarn is about the same diameter as dubbed thread, and when wrapped under tension, it flattens nicely to produce a smooth, tight, tapered foundation that's free of air pockets. Punch yarn is made by Plaid Enterprises (P.O. Box 7600, Norcross, GA 30091) and is sold primarily in craft stores on 225-yard cardboard mandrels. I wind it onto empty thread spools so I can run it from a bobbin to quickly build the foundation on any sizable nymph or streamer that calls for a dubbed body. To enhance the overall softness of the Woolly Worm, I also swap the traditional tail of stiff wool for a tuft of rabbit fur (cut from a hide or Zonker strip) that pulsates as the fly is drifted or stripped.

While genetic hen hackles are relatively long, they're not long enough to densely hackle an entire Woolly with a single feather, unless you use hackle that's grossly oversize. The solution is to palmer two feathers. To mirror the tapered profile of the dubbed body, I palmer a relatively small feather with short barbules over the rear of the body and a larger feather with longer barbules over the front of the body. Since the body is dubbed and hackled in two stages, it's a simple matter to switch color schemes at the midpoint. That quirk in the tying procedure became the inspiration for the Bi-Bugger, which is a unique, multicolored Soft-Hackle Woolly Bugger (described in the streamer section of this chapter).

The Soft-Hackle Woolly Worm in size 12 with a black body, black tail, and grizzly hackle is my bread-and-butter prospecting fly for Wisconsin streams, and it fishes well throughout the Rockies. For big western free-stone rivers, I tie the black and grizzly in size 6 to imitate big stonefly nymphs. For accurate presentations with light rods on small creeks, I tie the black and grizzly in size 16; it's a much smaller Woolly than you can readily buy, and even wary spring-creek trout often pounce on it.

My favorite color variation is all black with a hot orange tail. I often fish it in September, as brook and brown trout are gearing up for spawning and are becoming susceptible to bright attractor colors. Spring-spawning species also respond aggressively to the black and orange. It's also the best fly I've found for stripping just subsurface on alpine lakes, I think because the black body and hackle contrast sharply against the sky and are readily visible to fish from below.

On moving water, I usually rig with a putty strike indicator high on the leader butt and present the Woolly as a nymph—with an upstream cast and a dead drift. To fish snags and sweepers, I cast downstream and make a wet-fly swing across the face of the obstruction. On slow runs, I strip the fly. Given its combined nymph/wet-fly properties, there's not a current speed or angle of presentation that the Woolly can't handle. It's tremendously versatile for prospecting streams that have a mix of riffles, smooth runs, slack water, eddies, and snags.

Since the Soft-Hackle Woolly is tied quite differently than a standard Woolly, I've included complete tying instructions. I also tie my fly designs commercially and market them directly to anglers. To request a free mail-order fly catalog, write to Rich Osthoff, N6868 Sandstone Drive, Mauston, WI 53948.

Soft-Hackle Woolly Worm

Hook: Tiemco 5362 (3XL nymph hook).
Thread: 6/0.
Weight: 8 to 10 wraps of wire, same diameter as hook shank.
Tail: Tuft of rabbit fur.
Underbody: Punch embroidery yarn that roughly matches dubbing color.
Body: Rabbit dubbing; for added sparkle, add up to 20 percent Antron, but chop synthetic fibers very short so that they tease easily.
Hackle: 2 genetic hen hackles. (I primarily use Metz and Hoffman hen necks, but any genetic hen neck with feathers that are long enough for palmering is suitable.) Tie each hen hackle in by its tip. To avoid breaking the stem, wrap the first turn with light tension. On subsequent turns, the hackle stem should be firmly seated into the dubbing.

1. Wrap lead or nontoxic wire, and secure it with tying thread. Tie in the tail.
2. Wrap a forward-tapered yarn underbody and secure it by crisscrossing with tying thread. (I quickly wrap the yarn underbody using a second bobbin.)
3. Tie in the first hackle by the tip at the hook bend; barbule length should slightly exceed hook gap. Dub and palmer hackle over rear half of body.

4. Tie in the second hackle by the tip at the dubbing break; barbule length should be one and a half to two times the hook gap. Dub the front half of the body, and palmer the second hackle forward. Tie off the hackle and whip-finish the head.
5. Brush the finished fly from head to tail on all sides to sweep the hackle back, and marry it with teased-out dubbing fibers.

Scuds

Scuds are small freshwater crustaceans that thrive in cold, alkaline waters—just like trout do. Consequently, scud imitations are essential year-round prospecting "nymphs" on many of our most fertile spring creeks, tailwaters, and lakes.

In slow-moving or standing water with thick weed growth, scuds can number in the thousands per cubic foot. Trout often establish feeding stations around weed edges and openings and wait for scuds to wash or swim out. Scuds are fair swimmers, so even in current, I often experiment between a dead drift and stripping the fly just to see what trout respond to. On stillwater, stripping the fly definitely attracts fish and triggers strikes. On lakes, I also get many pickups on the drop, as the scud is sinking after the cast. Usually these takes can't be felt—you just have to scan the zone around the fly for the flash or form of a trout moving in. Casting from an elevated position allows you to see much deeper into the water, and that tactic has produced many of my best trout in high lakes. Golden trout, in particular, often charge a dropping scud, slam on the brakes, and sip in the fly. They hold it for only a second before spitting it out, and if you're not in position to see the take, you'll never know it happened.

Small scuds of the *Hyalella* genus can thrive in somewhat acidic waters and are important forage on many alpine lakes. Another small crustacean, the fairy shrimp, is even more common on high lakes. In fact, if a mountain lake has obese trout, you can just about bet that they got that way by chowing down on scuds or shrimp. Fairy shrimp resemble scuds, but they're much more transparent and they swim on their backs with their feet and gill filaments undulating upward. The Fast-Sinking Scud imitation that I designed for sight-casting to cruising trout on mountain lakes is actually a shrimp imitation. I dub a dense, oversize body from a fifty-fifty mix of rabbit and chopped Antron, and then brush the underbody to create resistance so that the fly flips onto its smooth shell-back and quickly sinks to the level of cruising fish. Brushing from under the fly up toward the edges of the shellback also flattens the body and projects soft dubbing fibers from the sides to nicely imitate swimming shrimp. To enhance the sink rate, I often fish the fly with about 5 feet of

4X tippet. In size 12, it casts like a bullet yet sinks quickly with minimal weight on the hook shank, making it perfect for sight-casting to cruisers. Big trout tend to cruise fast and close to bottom, and usually you get just one shot to sink a convincing fly in their path before they vanish. On high lakes, I've taken more good fish on the Fast-Sinking Scud than on all other flies combined.

Natural scuds, shrimp, and sow bugs (another crustacean that thrives in weedy spring flows) commonly range from size 12 to 16, although I've collected scuds below size 20. Scuds and sow bugs are usually olive to match vegetation. Shrimp are so transparent that you can clearly see their digestive tracts; olive and tan are common hues. However, the color and size of crustaceans vary among habitats, so it's always smart to collect a few naturals and then select imitations that are in the ballpark.

On many lakes, my Mega Scud has been the difference between boom and bust. It's essentially my Fast-Sinking Scud tied in bright orange with a silver flashback on a size 8 hook. I've never encountered natural fresh-water shrimp that big, or bright, or flashy, but trophy brook trout really pound this fly, and it's accounted for many fine goldens. The Mega Scud has such outstanding sinking characteristics that I can probe bottom in 10 to 15 feet of water, even when using a floating line. The fly remains highly visible to trout in deep or roiled water, so it's the scud I usually go to when fishing blind.

When removed from water, scuds curl into a defensive tuck, which leads many tiers to wrap their imitations on tightly curved hooks. In the water, however, scuds are fairly straight, and shrimp and sow bugs are even straighter, so I stick to a 1X long nymph/wet-fly hook (Tiemco 3761). Many tiers still cut crustacean shellbacks from clear poly, but Stretchrite clear elastic, sold in fabric stores, is much tougher. To emphasize segmentation, I rib my crustaceans under extremely heavy tension, using 3X to 5X tippet material, which is much stronger than the fine wire that most scuds are ribbed with, and I find that mono ribbing bites and holds much better on soft, textured elastic than on slippery poly.

Stoneflies

Stonefly nymph imitations are essential prospecting patterns on rocky western freestone river, where the heaviest populations of naturals occur. The biggest stoneflies live as nymphs for two to four years and shed their exoskeletons upward of twenty times as they grow to lengths exceeding 2 inches—a tantalizing mouthful even to a bruiser trout. Clean, cold, highly oxygenated western rivers like the Madison, Yellowstone, Middle Fork of the Salmon, and South Fork of the Flathead harbor tremendous numbers of nymphs in various sizes. The nymphs are poor swimmers that feed by crawling along the bottom in rocky riffles. When dislodged, they drift helplessly near the bottom until they can reattach, so an upstream cast with a dead drift along the bottom is usually the best presentation.

Many tiers mimic big stonefly nymphs with incredibly detailed, and rather stiff, patterns that are complex to tie. In my experience, softer, more impressionistic patterns perform at least as well, and since they're much simpler to tie, it's not a catastrophe to leave several hung in the rocks— where you should be fishing them. The Soft-Hackle Woolly Worm is my primary prospecting version. The Brooks Stone is another simple and effective nymph. Charles Brooks was a trophy trout chaser who specialized in dredging big western rivers with stonefly nymphs, and he designed his imitation in the round—with palmered thorax hackle and without a wing case—to minimize the appearance of tumbling in swift water, which he believed was a critical flaw in a stonefly nymph pattern.

Most bona fide stonefly patterns are tied on size 4 to 8 hooks to imitate the big species. Golden brown, dark brown, and black are the common body colors. Imitations run the gamut from realistic flies that look like they just crawled out from under a rock to attractor versions like the Montana Stone, with its yellow thorax, or the Bitch Creek, with its lively rubber tails and antennae. There are many species of small stoneflies for which the Soft-Hackle Woolly Worm and Fuzzy Hare's Ear are highly suggestive.

Beadhead Nymphs

Love 'em or despise 'em, beadheads are the rage in prospecting nymphs. Some fly fishers disparagingly refer to beadheads as "jigs" due to their nose-heavy design and fast-sinking characteristics, but the reflectivity of the bead is likely the more critical element. Most inedible debris in the drift is drab and opaque, while most edible organisms exhibit some degree of shine or translucency. Perhaps the highly reflective bead simply broadcasts to trout that this is something worth investigating. When the water is murky and you elect to stay with a small nymph, a flashy bead definitely boosts its visibility to trout.

Beadheads can be added to virtually any nymph or streamer, and some tiers do. If you catch more trout on beadheads, then fish 'em. After experimenting with beads, I haven't been compelled to add them to my regular prospecting nymphs. The beadhead that I use most is a simple caddis pupa dubbed on a curved hook, ribbed with copper wire, and then vigorously brushed to expand and blur the silhouette. The bead suggests the gas bubble that carries an ascending pupa to the surface. I once had a phenomenal few days on the upper Missouri by casting a size 16 cream version to riseforms; the trout took it just under the surface as an emerger. When I'm anticipating a caddis hatch within a couple hours, I often prospect deep with the Bead Caddis Pupa.

Bottom line: Many materials and tying techniques can impart the illusion of life to your prospecting nymphs, and the bead is one of them.

Squirrel Nymphs

Squirrel hair is exceptionally spiky stuff, and since I favor fuzzy, impressionistic nymphs, I frequently add squirrel to dubbing blends to boost guard hair density on Hare's Ears, Scuds, and other nymphs. Brushing a nymph vigorously really brings those guard hairs into play.

The two most common squirrels, gray and fox, furnish a range of important primary colors for simulating natural nymphs. The back hairs on both species are beautifully grizzled, especially on fox squirrel, which combines black, orange, and red into a rusty hue. Belly hair is white on gray squirrels and a gorgeous burnt tan on fox squirrels.

Dave Whitlock's Fox Squirrel Nymph is an excellent searching pattern that's tied primarily from squirrel. I tie the same design in a dark version using gray squirrel.

Pheasant-Tail Nymph

The Pheasant-Tail Nymph, or PT, is a definite high-water mark in nymph design. Pheasant tailfeathers perfectly imitate the olive-brown coloration and the subtle segmentation of many mayfly nymphs, right down to the fuzzy abdominal gills. Copper wire ribbing and a thorax of iridescent peacock herl add a lifelike sheen, while pheasant tail legs and tails are soft enough to impart some movement. In a range of sizes, the PT is great for prospecting and for matching active nymphs during hatches.

To imitate slender swimming nymphs like *Baetis*, tie the PT with an abbreviated wing case and just two strands of slender peacock herl for the thorax. To create a robust clinger-crawler profile, elongate the wing case to cover the front half of the hook shank, and wrap the thorax with four strands of fluffy peacock herl. Adding a flashback wing case improves the visibility of the fly for prospecting in off-color water or low light.

Soft-Hackle Wet Flies

Simple soft-hackle wet flies suggest an array of swimming, drowned, and emerging insects. Soft-hackles can be dead drifted, but they're really designed to be swung or pumped—and the capacity to be fished actively over a lot of water is often valuable in a prospecting fly. On moving water, I use soft-hackle wets primarily for across-and-down presentations when

I want to show trout something smaller and more subtle than a streamer. Wet flies are also outstanding for prospecting on lakes.

I suggest you add a few basic patterns to your nymph boxes. The versatile Partridge and Green matches many olive-bodied insects. Wets tied with plump peacock herl bodies are fine searching flies that stand out better than sparse ties in low light and murky water.

San Juan Worm

The San Juan Worm is big medicine for prospecting fertile tailwaters where true aquatic worms burrow into bottom sediments. Brazen tailwater trout have learned to line up just downstream from wading anglers and to chow down on worms and assorted nymphs as they're dislodged into the drift. Shuffling—the not-so-fine art of fishing to the trout that are feasting at your feet—is now illegal on most of the very tailwaters where it can be employed so effectively. I'll admit that early in the craze, I shuffled a bit for the novelty of it, but catching trout so automatically soon wore thin. After all, fly fishing isn't just about catching fish—it's about catching fish in a compelling fashion.

The San Juan Worm will always be linked to the dubious practice of shuffling, but it's a proven pattern for prospecting tailwaters with conventional nymphing techniques. The original San Juan Worm employs fine yarn wrapped tightly around a curved English baithook, which twists like a worm in current. More recent designs attach Ultra Chenille or chamois leather to a small nymph hook and allow the tail and head material to extend freely. Loose chamois moves and flexes beautifully in current and is my favorite worm material.

Aquatic worms aren't the only worms worth imitating. In farm country, I see drowned earthworms and night crawlers on stream bottoms after heavy rains. Inchworms and moth larvae are blown out of trees and into the drink, and a small tan or yellow Chamois Worm is a good imitation.

Black or dark brown chamois makes a remarkably fluid and convincing imitation of the common leeches that inhabit most trout water. Precut a chamois strip into a leech shape, and then lash it by the thorax to a small nymph hook, allowing the head and tail to extend freely. It's a great pattern for dead drifting; if you strip it, the head collapses back over the body.

Micronymphs

On extremely fertile tailwaters and spring creeks, even 5-pound trout routinely gorge on small organisms. Imitating the diminutive nymphs and larvae that are prevalent in the drift is often the key to steady action between hatches.

While spring creeks and tailwaters support a staggering quantity of trout forage, diversity is not usually that great. Midges and small multibrooded mayflies are the primary insect components, and I do most of my micronymphing with just two simple patterns.

The Pheasant Tail, or PT, Midge is my concoction. I use the same proven materials as in the Pheasant Tail Nymph—pheasant tail and copper wire—but I omit all appendages to imitate midge and free-swimming caddis larvae. Some waters are packed with small, dark microscuds that are too tiny to imitate with complex scud patterns, and the PT Midge is a workable match. I tie the PT Midge on size 16 to 24 dry-fly hooks by wrapping the abdomen and then the thorax from three or four continuous strands of pheasant tail. The strands are tied in near the bend by their tips, and as they're wrapped forward, the darker, thicker butts form a distinct thorax. The abdomen is ribbed with fine copper wire, which is tied off and snipped just prior to wrapping the thorax.

I was introduced to the Chocolate Emerger on the San Juan River, where it fished so well that I adopted it for other waters. It imitates swimming *Baetis* nymphs, which are staples on western spring creeks and tailwaters and are common to other trout waters. I tie it on size 18 and 20 dry-fly hooks. The tail is wood duck flank. Dub the abdomen and thorax from chocolate fur, or vary the color to match the prevailing naturals. Rib the abdomen with copper wire. Instead of a wing case, tie in gray Antron or Zelon yarn, and clip it short to suggest an emerging wing.

STREAMERS

On most trout water, prospecting with streamers produces more top-end trout than does any other tactic. Streamers can be tied to mimic baitfish, crayfish, leeches, and even small trout, or they can be loaded up with charisma and fished as attractors that provoke strikes out of aggression rather than hunger.

Big, meat-eating trout get that way by being efficient predators. They don't waste energy chasing everything in sight. They observe many potential victims, and then attack the most vulnerable. Suggestions of vulnerability can be built into streamers. Wounded baitfish swim erratically and transmit an unusual degree of flash, which triggers predatory attacks. I particularly like scaled or prismatic flash, which is nicely simulated by lively flash materials such as Fire Fly. A tuft of orange or red rabbit hair at the throat of a streamer suggests the flared gills of a dying baitfish. A bit of pink or red added to the back, belly, or tail of a streamer suggests bleeding or a fleshy wound.

Compared with other categories of flies, I carry a limited streamer selection, but the ones I tote pull regular duty.

Soft-Hackle Woolly Bugger

The Woolly Bugger seduces all kinds of game fish all over the map. It's simply a great prospecting fly that deserves its popularity. A well-tied Bugger has two things going for it that most streamers don't: It cuts a bold silhouette, even when viewed head-on. And it acts lively on a dead drift. The versatility to be fished up, across, or down, on a dead drift, swing, or strip with excellent movement and visibility makes it productive on all water types.

I tie Buggers in the same style as Woolly Worms—with soft, webby hen hackle and dubbed fur bodies that I brush vigorously (see the Soft-Hackle Woolly Worm for complete tying instructions). As good as the standard chenille-and-saddle-hackle Bugger is, a dubbed and brushed Soft-Hackle Bugger has a much stronger silhouette and vastly superior movement. Marabou is a tough material to beat for action, so I retain the traditional marabou tail. I use the tip of a marabou blood quill, plus about eight strands of flash material.

On Soft-Hackle Buggers, I palmer relatively long hackle over the thorax, at least double the hook gap. For hackling the front half of size 8 and larger Buggers, I usually use hen saddle or body feathers to achieve the desired hackle length, as it's getting tough to find long hackle on genetic hen necks.

An all black Soft-Hackle Bugger with silver flash is my go-to streamer for dirty or stained water; in murky depths, a black fly cuts a stronger, more opaque silhouette than a bright fly. For clear water, I like the Bi-Bugger, which is my mottled crayfish-sculpin color scheme: The tail is black over olive marabou, with gold flash, the rear of the body is olive with grizzly hackle, and the front is black with black hackle. The Soft-Hackle Bi-Bugger is so seductive that I don't reserve it for trout—it's also my top steelhead fly and my standard Bugger for smallmouth bass. Smallmouths and brown trout are particularly fond of crayfish, so I tie some Bi-Buggers with heavy metal eyes so that they can be hopped along the bottom. A head-heavy Bugger also plummets quickly in swift chutes to ride the productive bottom zone throughout a drift. Or it sinks a couple feet when hanging straight downstream on a tight line, so it's handy for probing under deadfalls. A white Bugger with silver flash appeals to trout that forage primarily on baitfish.

I often prospect small streams with a 4-weight rod and a size 12 Mini-Bugger, and it's on small streams, where I encounter lots of different water types in quick succession, that I really appreciate versatility of the Bugger. On medium-size streams, I usually go to size 8. On big rivers, I jump to size 4. I weight most buggers moderately, with about ten wraps of wire equivalent in diameter to the hook shank, to punch through the surface and start sinking on impact. To get down in very fast water, I add split shot to the tippet. Tying too much weight into streamers limits their versatility—and versatility is what Buggers are all about.

Muddler Minnow

The Muddler is my favorite swing fly for prospecting big western freestone rivers. Although it's designed to imitate bottom-hugging sculpins, I often swing a lightly weighted Muddler in the top half of the water column. That seems illogical until you consider that a healthy sculpin hugs the bottom like a suction cup and is supercamouflaged, whereas an injured or dying sculpin is buoyed upward by turbulence and is much more apparent and vulnerable to trout. A Muddler is also a ballpark imitation of an adult stonefly or grasshopper, both of which are usually taken by trout that are looking up.

The Muddler is commonly tied in marabou, Matuka, and fur strip variations, but the standard tie with turkey quill wings is still my workhorse. Normally I'm a fan of soft materials that pulsate on a dead drift, but I fish the Muddler mostly on downstream swings in strong current, where the rigid quill wings help it flutter and sweep enticingly, especially when the fly is tied with neutral buoyancy and fished on a sinking-tip line.

Most commercial Muddlers have long deer-hair collars that sandwich the wings. A Muddler tied like that has more bulk in the tail than in the head and is vertical in cross section. Real sculpins are flattened horizontally for hugging the bottom in current. They have fat heads and pronounced pectoral fins. To simulate the pectorals and maintain bulk up front, I tie my Muddler collars short and flare them sharply to the sides. Cow elk body hair has short, blunt tips that flare nicely.

To give a Muddler body more flash and substance, I scrap the traditional flat tinsel and wrap a stout oval body with Gold DMC embroidery thread, which I run from a bobbin. I don't weight the hook shank; the stout body and the streamer hook offset the hollow deer-hair head to give the fly the neutral buoyancy that I'm after.

I tie Muddlers on Tiemco 300 (6XL) streamer hooks. The extra shank length makes it easy to tie this fairly complex fly without crowding the various elements. Size 6 is good for all-around prospecting. Size 12 is handy on small streams.

Fur-Strip Streamers

Fur-strip streamers have remarkable prospecting powers and are easy to tie. Rabbit, the most common fur-strip material, is extremely soft and ripples beautifully on a dead drift or when stripped. Rabbit strips are available in a wide range of natural colors to imitate leeches and sculpins. Some natural colors, like natural brown and chinchilla, are nicely mottled. White rabbit is easily dyed to brilliant attractor colors like hot orange and chartreuse. Dark fur strips cut exceptionally strong silhouettes in deep water or low light, so they're great for dredging the bottom.

The Zonker is the most famous fur-strip streamer. It's tied in a range of natural and dyed colors for trout, steelhead, and salmon. Gary Borger's Strip Leech in black is the fur-strip pattern that I carry for trout. The Kiwi Muddler uses fur cut into a triangular wedge, rather than a straight strip, to suggest the forward taper of a sculpin. The Bunny Leech and various "roadkill" patterns are tied by wrapping a crosscut fur strip around the hook.

Fur-strip streamers are usually tied on big hooks, sizes 2/0 to 4, so when buying strips, select for long, thick hair that allows you to tie large patterns. For smaller patterns, long hair is easily plucked down to the desired length and density after the fly is tied.

Synthetic Hair Streamers

Some nifty and convincing baitfish imitations are being tied from synthetic hairs and furs that bristle with sheen and translucency and look very fishy in the water. Long-fibered synthetics can greatly enlarge the profile of a streamer without adding substantial weight, absorbency, or casting resistance. Hairs are easily layered in contrasting color bands to mimic the light bellies, flashy sides, and dark dorsals of baitfish. With experimentation, you're sure to find some uses for the new synthetic hairs in your own streamer fishing.

Various hairs have different properties, so play around. Ultra Hair, Big Fly Fiber, FisHair, and Craft Fur are all useful.

Noise Makers

Trout detect food in three ways: by scent, sight, and sound. As fly fishers, we sacrifice scent as an attractant. We primarily fixate on making our flies look convincing to trout. But sound is a big card we can play, especially at night, and streamers can be designed to create a ruckus.

Bass anglers tie their topwater bugs to pop, gurgle, and send out some vibes. My best night streamer for trout is adapted from a popular bass bug: the Dahlberg Diver. I tie a trout Diver on a size 10, 3XL hook with a dark deer-hair body and marabou tail to stand out against the night sky, and I add plenty of flash to the tail to help suggest a struggling baitfish. I've used a Diver to take as many as ten trout on a single run. And I've seen a Diver do zip on pools that I know were loaded with trout, including some big ones. You just have to put it out there and see how trout respond on a given night. When it's too dark to fish small stuff, you really have nothing to lose by knotting on a big streamer and making some noise.

Bobbing Baitfish

The Bobbing Baitfish is a buoyant, foam-filled Mylar minnow that shines on lakes for all game fish. In fact, it was the fly's impressive performance on walleyes and hefty smallmouth bass that led me to try it on trout lakes. I primarily run the Baitfish on sinking lines that belly below the fly. When stripped, the fly dives to follow the path of the line. Between strips, the fly buoys upward, rather than dropping as a neutral or weighted streamer does. Since the Baitfish rises on the pause, it's great for fishing in close contact to rocky bottoms and weed beds without constantly fouling. When trout are cruising shallow, I run the Baitfish just below the surface, and at times I use it to prospect for suspended fish. But as a buoyant streamer, it's uniquely suited for efficiently prospecting on the bottom.

Lakes have tremendous water volume compared with streams, and even on the best lakes, most water is fishless. For prospecting stillwater, I like streamers that exude a tremendous amount of flash to pull fish in from a distance, and mylar tubing does that. As a hard-bodied fly, the Baitfish also wobbles and transmits vibrations that fish detect. The harder the Baitfish is stripped, the more erratic it behaves, which makes it ideal for ripping through big water.

The Baitfish doesn't dazzle everybody right out of the gate. You have to develop a feel for working it, especially close to the bottom. I can feel the belly of a sinking line sliding on the bottom, and I can feel the fly bump rocks—that's when I end the strip. Fish often take the fly as it's rising on the pause, and as I begin to strip, I can detect the presence of a fish before it feels alarming line pressure and spits out the fly. On lakes where trout and other game fish forage primarily for baitfish, it's the first and often the only streamer I reach for.

Many streamers are tedious to tie, but I can wrap nearly twenty Baitfish in an hour. I tie the pattern on 6XL streamer hooks in sizes 2, 6, and 12, using $3/8$-, $1/4$-, and $1/8$-inch-diameter mylar tubing, respectively. I stick to silver, gold, or pearl tubing, although other colors are available. Since the Baitfish is tied with an unusual technique, detailed tying instructions are given here.

Bobbing Baitfish

Hook:	Tiemco 300 6XL.
Thread:	Flat-waxed nylon.
Tail:	Even tips of a marabou blood quill.
Underbody:	Buoyant closed-cell foam.
Body:	Mylar tubing; the finished body is coated with five-minute epoxy.
Eyes:	Doll eyes.

1. Cut a humpback foam underbody that's as long as the hook shank (a size 2 underbody is 1¹/₂ inches long, ¹/₂ inch high and ¹/₈ inch thick).
2. Lash the foam underbody to the top of the hook shank, using criss-crossing thread wraps. Compress and bind the foam securely to the shank at the head and tail.
3. Cut a section of mylar tubing that's slightly longer than the hook shank, and remove the cotton core. Tie in the hollow tubing just behind the hook eye, so that it projects forward over the eye. Half-hitch and snip the thread.
4. Roll the tubing backward over the foam underbody (the tubing turns inside out as it's rolled).
5. Reattach the thread at the hook bend while pulling rearward on the mylar tubing to stretch it taut.
6. Trim excess tubing. Tie in the marabou tail, and whip-finish.

I use black and olive markers to stripe and darken the dorsal surfaces before coating the entire mylar body with five-minute epoxy. Doll eyes are added while the epoxy is still tacky. Big doll eyes make the fly rise head-first so that it flips erratically at the start of each dive.

DRY FLIES
Dry flies for prospecting fall into two categories. Some are purely attractors, whereas others have crossover value for prospecting and imitating natural organisms.

Attractor drys are typically big, high-floating, and gaudy—they bear little resemblance to anything in nature. They're designed to get noticed by fish and to be easy for anglers to track on the surface. Attractors are in their element on fast water, where trout don't have all day to study the fly, and in lightly fished backcountry where trout aren't conditioned to inspect flies carefully.

Smaller, naturally colored drys that imitate common food forms are usually the best bets for prospecting on smooth or heavily fished waters where trout have the time and inclination to eyeball offerings critically before committing.

Regardless of where you fish, packing attractor and imitative drys will make you more versatile. For example, on spring creeks and tailwaters where trout are too selective to consistently fall for big attractors in daylight, those same flies can suddenly sizzle at dark, when they're readily located by trout. And while stunted trout living in overcrowded alpine lakes usually attack attractor drys, trophy lake fish living in balance with their food supply can be maddeningly selective, even between hatches. I've found that when the wind drops on wilderness lakes and big, wary trout get a perfect view of my offering, a prospecting dry that looks darned natural is often required in order to seal the deal.

Wulffs

I'd wager that the Royal Wulff has seen more float time than any other attractor dry fly. Lee Wulff designed the Royal Wulff to be eye candy to trout—a sort of strawberry-and-whipped-cream temptation—and he succeeded big-time. Peacock herl, the principal body component, has universal appeal to trout. The dark body and dense brown hackle present a strong silhouette to trout that are looking up, while the contrasting white calf-tail wings make the fly easy for anglers to track. The Wulff is heavily hackled and has a stiff hair tail to float well and take a beating.

Big, bushy Wulffs still have some applications, but small, sparse versions have become more useful. I tie most of my Wulffs in sizes 12 and 16, with sparser wings, tail, and hackle than the original. Calf body hair stacks nicely for winging small Wulffs. Moose body hair produces a strong, sparse tail. The Wulff I use the most is a toned-down color variation that I call the Hare's Ear Wulff. I tie it with dun wings, grizzly saddle hackle, and Hare's Ear dubbing.

Industrial-Strength Dun

Attractor drys like Humpies, Trudes, and Wulffs have long been mainstays for prospecting the swift freestone rivers of the Rockies, but as angling pressure has skyrocketed, the effectiveness of many attractors has nosedived. When I began to see frequent refusals to Wulffs, I countered with my Industrial-Strength Dun. It's a Wulff-grade dry fly with a more convincing mayfly wing silhouette. The wing is a pair of broad, webby hen saddle hackle tips tied in upright with their concave surfaces abutting. I dab some Flexament between the wing feathers and stroke them upright to lock them into a single upright wing.

The Industrial-Strength Adams has become my favorite hackled dry for prospecting big freestone rivers. It has a grizzly wing, mixed grizzly and brown saddle hackle, dark gray dubbing, and a moose body tail. In other color variations, I use the same design for matching green drakes and other large mayfly duns.

Classic Dry Flies

As flush-floating, no-hackle designs have proliferated, hackled drys have fallen from favor for fooling selective trout during hatches. But on windy days when natural duns are being buffeted about, a hackled fly can still be the best match. And for prospecting, hackled drys are more visible to trout and easier for anglers to track.

The Adams is a dry with definite crossover capability. In a range of sizes, it gives you a workable match for most dark-bodied mayfly duns. And the mottled grizzly-brown-gray color scheme has proven prospecting powers. The Gray Fox, with its mixed grizzly-ginger color scheme, is an excellent light-colored prospecting alternative to the darker Adams.

Mayfly Spinners

A rusty mayfly spinner with Antron wings is valuable for prospecting demanding spring creeks and tailwaters in the waning light just before full dark. That's a time when natural spinners often fall, so fish are likely to be receptive, even if there aren't naturals afloat. Experience has convinced me that right at dark, even a small size 18 spinner imitation lying spread-eagle in the film remains quite visible to trout. Many times, by switching to a spinner, I've been able to milk a few extra fish, including some big ones, while a glimmer of light remained and it was still possible to see sipping rises.

Elk Hair Caddis

I prospect more with an Elk Hair Caddis than with any other dry. Caddis are abundant on most trout waters, and adult caddis can hang around for several weeks, so trout get used to grabbing them opportunistically. The Elk Hair Caddis also suggests small stoneflies, large midges, and immature hoppers, which certainly broadens its appeal.

Streams that harbor loads of pan-size fish are fun to prospect with a dry fly, and a well-tied Elk Caddis can stand up to at least a couple dozen fish and still float enticingly. Palmered hackle has superior skating properties, making the fly well suited for prospecting on lakes. I hackle my Elk

Caddis more simply than the original Troth version, tying in the hackle by the stem at the bend, palmering it forward over the body, and omitting the wire ribbing.

A color variation I use a lot is my Grizzly Caddis. It has a natural elk-hair wing, gray body, and grizzly hackle. In a fly that's so conducive to skating, I think that mottled grizzly hackle helps suggest wings in motion.

Upland Caddis

Many anglers who are sticklers for precisely matching mayfly duns in color, silhouette, and size carry only a couple patterns in a few basic colors for matching all adult caddis. That's perplexing, since caddis are more common and prolific than mayflies, live longer in the adult stage, and occur in a much wider range of colors.

The Upland Caddis gives me the ability to precisely match any caddis adult. The tent-wing silhouette is a dead ringer for the natural, while body feathers from a variety of upland gamebirds, and some waterfowl, capture the rich coloration and mottling of real caddis wings. During many caddis hatches, trout key on emerging pupae. Adult caddis patterns really come into their own as prospecting drys. On high-gradient streams, I usually prospect with a tough, buoyant Elk Hair Caddis, but on smooth spring creeks, tailwaters, and lakes, where savvy trout get an undistorted look, the highly convincing Upland Caddis really earns its keep. It's the fly I often go to during caddis season when I spot a nice fish rising sporadically between hatches. And it shines for just searching good caddis waters.

I build the wing assembly off the hook and lash it to a dubbed and hackled body. Building the wings is a technique you can learn in an evening, and once you have it down, the rest of the fly is a cinch. Start by peeling the fluff from the base of two body feathers. Then apply a couple drops of Flexament, and stroke each feather from butt to tip until it locks into a streamlined shape.

To assemble the two streamlined feathers into a single tent wing, pinch them between a thumb and forefinger with the stem butts criss-crossing. With your other thumb and forefinger, pinch the feather tips together so that the two feathers abut along their inside edges to form a spine. Practice aligning and pinching a set of feathers into a tent wing until you can do it easily. Once you have that down, bonding the feathers is easy. Simply maintain your pinch on the stem butts while you apply Flexament to the inside edge of each feather. Then pinch the feather tips together and hold them until they bond along the spine, which takes about ten seconds. The crisscrossing stem butts become the antennae and are trimmed to length after the fly is tied. I often build a big batch of tent wings one night and tie flies the following night.

To complete the fly, dub and hackle a caddis body. For skating the fly on lakes, I palmer the hackle. For moving water, I hackle at the thorax. Either way, trim the hackle flush with the top of the body so that the tent wing sits low. To tie in the wing assembly, catch it with the thread right where the stem butts cross. I dub a bit of fur over the tie-in point and lift the antennae to whip-finish under them. While the fly is still in the vise, cut the tent wing to the desired length, cutting it at a 45-degree angle to form a V-notch at the rear of the canopy.

Here are the Upland Caddis colors that I fish most frequently and the feathers that I tie them with: light tan hen pheasant breast, dark tan bobwhite quail back, mottled brown ruffed grouse or Hungarian partridge back, mottled gray Hungarian partridge breast, solid gray chukar partridge back, burnt orange woodcock breast, black wood duck back. By working with a variety of upland and waterfowl feathers, you can select the precise color and mottling of your local caddis.

Midges

On tailwaters, midge imitations are essential for prospecting back eddies and slow water. Even between obvious midge hatches, some trout rise sporadically in these areas, and they're less suspicious of midge imitations than of bigger drys. The sheer abundance of fish in fertile tailwaters assures that your tiny offering is seen on most drifts.

The Griffith's Gnat is tied with peacock herl and palmered grizzly hackle to imitate large midges and mating clusters of small midges. To better imitate small individual midges, I tie my Topwater Midge down to size 24. The body is three strands of pheasant tail tied in by the tips and wrapped forward. Take a couple turns of grizzly hackle at the thorax, and trim the hackle on the bottom so the fly sits flush on the water. The color scheme resembles the Griffith's Gnat, but the Topwater Midge is much less bulky.

Grasshoppers

I've seen trout move farther to nail a hopper imitation than any other dry fly. That's not surprising, given that hoppers are big enough to be readily seen (and heard) by trout and that they represent a substantial meal.

There are many good hopper patterns. The best of the bunch are no-hackle patterns that sit low in the water like the stout-bodied naturals. Many tiers strive for realism in their hopper patterns, right down to prominent rear legs. I omit the legs altogether and tie a distress-style hopper with a flared elk-hair collar over a cock pheasant saddle feather to imitate partially opened wings. Clipped elk-hair heads are tougher than clipped deer hair, and elk is a bit darker and more natural in tone. Natural hopper bodies are often tinted yellow, but they're not hot yellow, so I tie bodies from green foam and rib them with yellow floss. On heavily fished spring creeks and tailwaters, I drop to size 12, which is significantly smaller than what most anglers toss. Trout that have been pounded with hopper imitations often take toned-down, scaled-down patterns more decisively.

On many watersheds, hopper time is the only time that you can prospect with a dry fly and have a legitimate shot at taking trophy trout.

Warm summer winds flush hoppers from streamside vegetation. Hopper-seeking trout often lie tight to grassy banks.

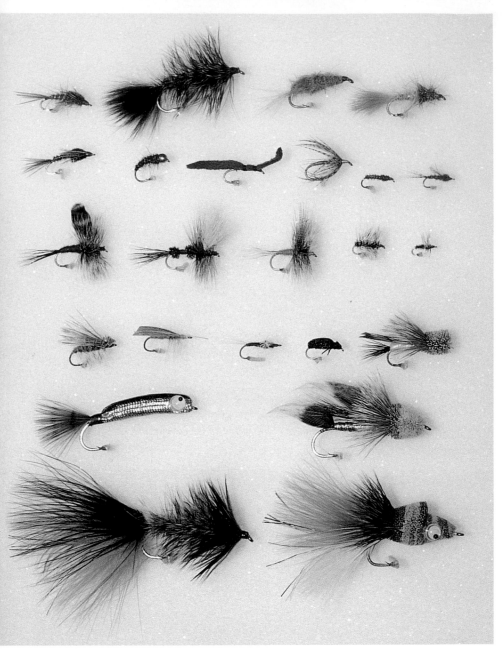

Many of the author's favorite prospecting flies are his own designs or variations of established patterns. **Top row:** *(left to right) Chocolate Hare's Ear, Soft Hackle Woolly Worm, Fast-Sinking Scud, Fox Squirrel Nymph.* **Second Row:** *Pheasant Tail Nymph, Bead Caddis Pupa, Chamois Leech, Soft-Hackle Wet Fly, Pheasant Tail Midge, Chocolate Emerger.* **Third Row:** *Industrial Strength Adams, Royal Wulff, March Brown, Griffith's Gnat, Topwater Midge.* **Fourth Row:** *Grizzly Caddis, Upland Caddis, Rusty Spinner, Foam Beetle, Distress Hopper.* **Fifth Row:** *Bobbing Baitfish, Muddler Minnow.* **Bottom Row:** *Soft-Hackle Bi-Bugger, Deerhair Diver. (All flies tied by Rich Osthoff.)* PHOTO BY PAUL BAKER

The author's brother, Eric, plays one of several nice brown trout that he micro-nymphed from a deep, slow refuge run.

In mid-summer, rainy or overcast days often produce great midday fishing. The author's sister-in-law, Neysa, nymphed this big brown at high noon in July.

Utah's Green River is one of the most crowded tailwaters in the West. Yet, the author routinely enjoys great fishing and solitude by hiking over high bluffs and then descending to fish remote canyon stretches.

On the warm, sunny days of spring, trout are on the prowl from mid-morning right into evening, hatch or no hatch. The author took this early-April brown by long-line nymphing to the far bank of this big pool.

On frigid high-altitude lakes, the best fishing is often on sunny summer days when sunlight activates the food chain and spotting conditions are ideal. The author took this big Wyoming golden trout on a sunny August afternoon.

Powerful thunderstorms turn streams into muddy torrents. Note the flood debris piled atop this stream bank. But as the water drops and begins to clear, the fishing is often superb.

Big, predatory trout often ambush baitfish in the shallow tails of runs. The author nymphed this 25-inch brown from shallow water on a small Wisconsin spring creek.

In summer, the daybreak fishing on tailwater rivers is often spectacular, while competition from other anglers is nil. The author displays one of many fine rainbows he took before sunup on New Mexico's San Juan River.

Soft-Hackle Buggers are tremendously versatile streamers that can be dead-drifted, stripped, or fished on a conventional streamer swing. And they can be counted on to consistently move big, predatory trout

On small streams, lunker structures such as this one can create an artificial cutbank that provides trout with critical escape cover. The author's rod and vest are sitting on one of the large rocks that are typically used to anchor these submerged wooden structures.

Swift, clear freestone rivers, such as Idaho's Middle Fork of the Salmon, are tailor-made for prospecting with attractor dry flies and streamers. Trout have to take quickly or go hungry.

Mature browns often spend the winter and spring in degraded lower watersheds where trout densities are low but baitfish thrive. Eric Osthoff landed this fine brown from a stream section that is generally considered to be sucker water.

PART THREE

Special Situations

Chapter 8

Beating
the Heat

Summer isn't just hot, it's long. Throughout the East and the Midwest, trout fishers contend with heat from June into September—or for roughly half the trout season. Many anglers respond to hot weather and rising water temperatures by reducing their fishing time, but with the right strategies, you can torque the rod right through the dog days. A few of the points discussed in this chapter have been mentioned previously, but they bear repeating as important considerations in hot-weather strategies.

TARGET THE COOL STREAMS

Just because the weather is simmering doesn't mean that all of your local streams are. Cool water can still be found high in watersheds and close to concentrated spring sources. When summer really clamps down, the most significant adjustment you can make is to head upstream to cool headwaters, where trout feed actively through the hot, sunny hours. The headwater sections of many spring creeks peak at 62 to 64 degrees on the hottest days, and those are ideal feeding temperatures.

Anglers who prowl the headwaters not only find active trout, but encounter fresh concentrations of trout that have moved upstream in search of cool water. Headwaters are small-fish habitat for much of the year, but as summer redistributes the trout population, some big fish suddenly show up in small water. Active fish, lots of fish, some big fish—that's what cool headwater tributaries can deliver when main stems are running tepid.

On small headwaters, good holding water is usually scattered. Since few anglers are willing to battle heat and lush summer growth to cover long stretches of stream, you can ply most headwaters in virtual solitude all summer long. It's like owning private water without the taxes. On some of the best hot-weather creeks in southern Wisconsin, I rarely see another angler or even a boot print. Yet the big, well-trodden catch-and-release streams within a few miles draw crowds all summer, even when they're running at 70 degrees and fishing marginally. This occurs in a region that has wide-open stream access laws and dozens of lightly fished spring creeks with solid populations of wild trout. Chicago, Minneapolis, and Milwaukee are all within a three-hour drive of southwestern Wisconsin, and any fly fisher who puts some sweat equity into exploring the region is going to discover some dependable hot-weather streams. That's probably the case in most regions with significant amounts of free-flowing trout water. Before you trim your expectations or throw in the towel on hot-weather trout, make sure you're fishing the coolest streams in your region. Those are likely to be different streams, or at least different sections, than you're fishing in May, so be ready to do some exploring.

Big tailwater rivers are largely immune to the effects of hot weather. I've fished the San Juan River in fierce August heat, yet the water remained so cold that my feet eventually went numb inside my neoprene waders.

TAKE ADVANTAGE OF GRADIENT
Headwaters have another thing going for them in summer that most anglers overlook: They have relatively high gradient with lots of riffles and well-oxygenated water. Where oxygen levels are high, trout remain surprisingly active at high temperatures. I've had very steady action in 68- to 71-degree water by ignoring slack water and targeting pockets directly below riffles.

Even trout that are drawn to well-oxygenated water don't battle current needlessly. They seek slow cushions along the bottom, against banks, or behind boulders. The best presentation is usually a dead-drifted nymph that's weighted to get down quickly.

BEYOND BANKER'S HOURS
When you're fishing streams that peak at 70 degrees or slightly higher, you want to target the cool hours. Streams are coolest at dawn. Even on days that are destined to sizzle, you'll usually see comfortable water temperatures from daybreak into midmorning, typically about 5 degrees cooler than the afternoon highs. If you can roust yourself out of the sack you can cover a lot of water before it heats up.

Most anglers opt to fish summer evenings over mornings—probably because they're already awake. Flying insects are more active in the evening, so you're likely to see at least sporadic surface activity, but during heat waves, most of the cooling in the daily cycle comes well after sundown. When the dog days arrive, I put the bulk of my daylight effort into mornings instead of evenings, because I'm guaranteed a much longer window of significantly cooler water.

Night fishing really comes into its own in summer. In early summer, streams cool rapidly after sundown, and you may catch a flurry of activity by extending your fishing for just an hour or two after dark. By late summer, the water may not cool significantly until well after midnight, and you're better off fishing the predawn hours and into daylight. In summer, big, carnivorous trout often prowl under cover of darkness—a topic discussed in chapter 10.

PLAY THE SHADE

Streams that run through woodlands heat more slowly and peak at cooler temperatures than neighboring meadow streams. The difference in peak temperature might be only a few degrees, but trout in woodland streams feed longer in the mornings, turn on earlier in the evenings, and remain more aggressive at midday. Extremely hot weather often coincides with low, clear water and very spooky trout. If you work in shade, you won't cast a shadow, and you'll avoid fish-spooking glare from your rod, line, and clothing.

In open country, be on the lookout for stream sections that pick up shade a couple hours earlier than the surrounding water. That happens regularly where streams swing tight to bluffs or canyon walls. In vertical terrain, north-south-flowing stream sections take less direct sunlight than east-west-flowing waters, and the difference can be many hours per day. I first noticed that disparity while fishing deep river canyons in the Rockies, and now I regularly take advantage of prolonged shade on hill-country streams around home.

Many streams flow into and out of direct sunlight at frequent intervals. Since their water is moving and mixing, temperatures are similar in the sun and the shade. But the comfort level of trout is still greater in shade, because they're not absorbing direct solar energy. You'll also be much more comfortable fishing in shade, even if the air temperature is just slightly cooler than in the sun.

MAKE DEEP, DELIBERATE PRESENTATIONS
WITH SMALL OFFERINGS

As water temperatures approach 70 degrees, trout become less active and seek cushions in the current where they can hold with little effort. Nine times out of ten, that's on the bottom in the deepest runs. To catch inactive trout, you usually want to put a nymph right at their level on a deliberate, drag-free drift. Sluggish trout are often more interested in tidbits than in mouthfuls. Where I prospect with a size 12 nymph in May, I often drop to a size 16 in August. Micronymphing is an essential hot-weather technique.

TARGET HIGH-DENSITY WATERS
All trout in a population don't respond to heat in the same way. Some feed more actively than others at 68 degrees. When water temperatures are marginal, target streams that have dense fish populations, even if that means pursuing pan-size trout rather than lunkers. In a stream that's loaded with trout, there's a level of competition that spurs some fish to feed even at uncomfortable temperatures.

STAY COOL AND HYDRATED
Extreme heat and humidity are tough to fish through, but you can make some adjustments to stay cool.

Trade your waders for hip boots, unless hippers just don't allow you to get into good casting position on most runs. Hippers are much cooler and less tiring to walk in. I'm constantly amazed by the numbers of anglers who wear chest waders on small streams where they're not needed.

Even some big freestone rivers, like the Madison, can be worked quite effectively in hippers, because active fish gravitate toward the banks to feed. At prime time, most anglers in chest waders are standing where they should be fishing. Granted, rivers have deep runs where hippers are a disadvantage. But hippers extend your comfortable walking range by many miles a day, allowing you to prospect more productive bank water and get away from other anglers to reach undisturbed fish. That kind of mobility can be worth far more than the extra 18 inches of freeboard that waders provide. When it's time to make the long walk back to the car or camp, just roll your hippers below your knees and hike in comfort.

Nylon tackle packs are lighter than fishing vests and much more comfortable in summer. For years, I resisted tackle packs and clung to my vest. Then I tried a waistpack with a nifty design and the right capacity for my needs. I like it so well that my vest has been relegated to deep-wading duty only.

Dark clothing absorbs the sun's rays, and bright, reflective clothing spooks fish. Muted tans and greens blend with the landscape and don't absorb excessive heat, making them good compromise colors, especially for hats and shirts, which are the two garments most visible to fish.

Prolonged exposure to direct sunlight saps you of energy and speeds dehydration. The more skin you cover, the better. Long shirt sleeves and a cap with a circular brim or neck flap are essentials.

Choose lightweight, breathable fabrics. For many summers, I fished in 100 percent cotton long-sleeve T-shirts; cotton-polyester blends aren't nearly as comfortable. Vented nylon shirts and pants designed for tropical flats fishing are great for summer trouting. Nylon blends, like Supplex, are incredibly lightweight yet very abrasion and rot resistant, so they last for several seasons, more than justifying their cost.

To stay cool, stay wet. Dunk your shirt sleeves and hat frequently. Wear a wet bandanna around your neck. Keeping your head, arms, and shoulders wet has a tremendous cooling effect equivalent to wet wading, yet you're not beating up your feet by slogging for miles in soggy boots or exposing your legs to chiggers, leeches, snakes, and poisonous plants. When I have a long walk back to the car, I wet down just before leaving the stream.

At the end of a long, hot session of intense fishing, a dip in trout water is bracing. A towel and swim trunks are just wet stuff to carry. Peel down away from the road and take the plunge. Use your bandanna for light toweling as you air dry. If you'll be camping out and fishing the next day, you'll sleep more soundly with the salt and grime rinsed from your body.

I keep several gallons of water in my car so that I have plenty to pour over my head. Rather than dumping 10 pounds of ice cubes in my cooler, I use three frozen half-gallon water jugs. As the jugs slowly melt over a few days, I have a steady supply of ice water to drink.

Drink plenty of water at frequent intervals. In heat, you dehydrate faster than you realize, and if you don't replace lost fluids, you fatigue quickly and are prone to headaches. Even when I expect to fish for just a few hours, I carry a pint of water. If I'll be away from the car or camp all day, I pack a water filter. In a full day of fishing and hiking, I often drink about 3 quarts of water a day, especially in the arid West; packing a filter shaves 6 pounds or more in water weight. If you'll be drinking anything but spring water right from a bubbling source, use a water filter that removes bacteria and viruses, normally classified as a water purifier.

On a scorching afternoon, there's nothing more compelling than a wild, little trout stream—to wade its course, to feel its cool transparent push, to dunk your head, and to stiffen at the icy rivulets racing down your spine. The hotter the day is, the better it all feels.

And there's a special satisfaction in catching moody, hot-weather trout. Everybody has banner days in May. August is the test of how well you know your local waters and how adaptable you are.

Chapter 9

Dealing with Dirty Water

There are two types of dirty water: There's the high, chocolate stuff that transforms streams and rivers into rushing torrents and shuts the fishing down, and there are varying degrees of off-colored water that can actually work in an angler's favor.

AVOID THE REALLY DIRTY STUFF

The best way to counter extremely high, dirty water is to head elsewhere. When a powerful storm dumps several inches of rain on your fishing plans, it pays to be familiar with many streams, rather than just a pet few, because streams drop and clear at different rates.

The same headwater streams that remain cool in midsummer are often the first to clear. Since headwaters sit at the tops of watersheds and drain relatively small areas, storm surges pass quickly. Narrow headwater ravines aren't usually farmed as intensively as broad lower valleys, which means less siltation and discoloration when it does rain. When the larger streams in southern Wisconsin are running way off-color, I often select a small headwater stream and hike it right to its spring sources. It's a good excuse to explore some roadless valley that's rarely fished. Even small woodland streams tend to have scattered deep runs where trout congregate. By walking the entire stream course, I locate the best brook trout runs, and I know right where to head in fall when nice browns from downstream are pushing upstream to spawn.

In heavily forested regions, absorption of rainwater is excellent, and runoff carries very little silt. In Wisconsin, our largest trout rivers are in the central and northern forests, and while these rivers run high during heavy rains, they remain much cleaner than farm-country streams. I once fished the upper St. Joe River in the Idaho Panhandle during a wet week. One night, rain drummed so hard and so long that I was worried about flash flooding, and I was certain that the river would be unfishable, but at daybreak I was amazed to discover that the river hadn't risen or colored perceptibly. The lush forest in the river corridor had soaked up the deluge like a giant sponge.

In the vast watersheds of the West, a single dirty tributary can muck up an otherwise clean river. That's the case where the Lamar River meets the Yellowstone River near the head of the Black Canyon in Yellowstone Park. The upper Lamar has dirt banks up to 100 feet high. When it rains hard, the Lamar runs chocolate, and its payload of dirt eventually reaches the Yellowstone and shuts down the fishing from the Black Canyon downstream. I've been fishing the Black Canyon in bluebird weather when the Yellowstone has gone from clear to unfishable within minutes—a sure sign of earlier thunderstorms on the Lamar. Yet the Yellowstone above the Black Canyon, and other area streams, remained clear.

I ran into a similar situation while backpacking along Idaho's Big Creek, which is a major tributary to the Middle Fork of the Salmon. I started fishing high on Big Creek and worked my way downstream for 20 miles over several days. The cutthroats were cooperating until the skies opened up. When the rains ended, Big Creek ran the color of white chocolate, and the fishing was obviously done for a while. I broke camp and started hiking upstream, with the intention of blowing all the way out to the trailhead that day, but halfway back, I passed the mouth of Monumental Creek and discovered that it was the culprit. Above the mouth of Monumental, Big Creek still ran clear as a bell, and I ended up fishing for another two days. A few days later, I backpacked high into the Monumental Creek drainage to fish a remote lake that was rumored to hold trophy cutts. En route, I crossed several acres of mud flows that must have resulted from landslides. When it rained hard, that exposed mud was discoloring the entire drainage for some 30 miles downstream. Lakes are rarely discolored by rain, and even though it poured on that trip, I hit clear water and good fishing at the cutthroat lake.

If lightning isn't cracking, the start of a rainstorm is an ideal time to prospect. As the water rises and forage increases in the drift, trout gorge unselectively. With luck, the rain tapers off before the water turns muddy, and trout continue to feed aggressively for several hours. That's a common scenario during the soft, intermittent rains of spring. But if the clouds unleash a real gully washer, the fast fishing on the front end of a storm is short-lived, and it can easily be a couple days before a given stream is fishable again.

When you look at a muddy stream raging far out of its banks, it's difficult to believe that trout can survive, but survive they do, by hunkering down in the stream channel. Even during a flood, hydraulic friction reduces current speed close to the banks and bottom. Those are the primary structures that trout hug until the water drops. Boulders, bridge pilings, and other obstructions that break the current are also high-water havens.

During floods, trout are preoccupied with escaping the brunt of the current. Significant feeding doesn't resume until flows recede and silt begins to settle out. By then, trout have been off their feed for a day or more, and they're hungry if water temperatures are anywhere near optimal. It's prime time to prospect if you use the right tactics.

MAKE SLOW, DEEP PRESENTATIONS

As streams just begin to clear, trout are still hugging structure. Dry flies are out. Weighted nymphs and streamers are in. Presentations should be tight to the bottom, banks, and other structure. When visibility is only a foot or two, trout have little time to spot and react to a passing fly. The slower your presentation, the better.

On upstream presentations, fish a short line and strive for an absolute dead drift right along bottom. Make a very deliberate pickup at the end of the drift—that generates a lot of dirty water strikes, probably because lifting the fly vertically differentiates it from the murky background, yet trout can still grab it without leaving the slow cushion of water along the bottom.

If visibility is poor, even a dead drift may move the fly past fish too quickly. If you're not getting strikes where you should be, try working the fly downstream on a tight line. Weight the fly so that it plummets swiftly to the bottom. Repeatedly lift the fly a foot or two off the bottom, and then let it slip downstream for a couple feet as it sinks. If the streambanks are wide open, you can walk the fly downstream, like a dog on a leash, probing around every interesting obstacle and covering water very efficiently with a minimum of casting. Since your fly is moving slower than the current, trout have time to see it and grab it before it passes.

Probe dirty runs thoroughly. Make lots of casts to confined areas. Alter your position slightly between casts, until you achieve a slow drift along the bottom in each promising slot. When you get a strike, stay put and replicate your drift exactly—you may be into a pod of trout that are crowded into a small depression. Once you locate the sweet spot in a run, the dirty water will cover your movements as you play and release fish, and you can go on a hot streak.

If you're getting your fly down where it should be, you'll hang frequently on invisible rubble. Check your hook point regularly, and sharpen it as needed. When you snag the bottom in clear water, you usually have to bust off the fly to avoid disturbing an entire run, but in dirty water, just wade close to the fly, quietly work it free, and resume fishing. You can still hook nearby trout that are oblivious to your presence.

DRIFT BIG, DARK FLIES
The dirtier the water is, the bigger and darker your nymph or streamer should be. Big flies are easier to see than small flies, and dark flies maintain a strong silhouette in dirty water.

Adding some flash material makes flies more visible and differentiates them from inedible debris in the drift—and there's plenty of trash in the wake of a storm. Soft, buggy materials also enhance the silhouette and liveliness of your flies. Trout are rarely selective as they resume feeding after a spate, so it's a time to go big and ugly to be sure your fly gets noticed.

GET CLOSE
Trout in dirty water are very approachable, and that's a huge card to play. Getting close to your target water allows you to fish a very short line, or just the leader. Short-line presentations translate into deep, drag-free drifts that are difficult to replicate with a long line in clear conditions.

When the water is dirty, you can stand right over bottom-hugging trout and work them with remarkable precision and efficiency. You can fish from high banks and exposed positions where you'd normally stick out like King Kong. You can march right into brushy pockets where you can't cast and just lower the fly. If you know the whereabouts of a lunker that has grown old by dwelling in an unapproachable lie, this is the time to slip through his defenses and drop a big, juicy morsel right in his bread box.

When the water is dirty, wading quietly is more critical than ever. With a silent approach, you can slip within a rod length of trout and show them that perfect dead drift. Be on the lookout for slots and pockets that are difficult to approach in clear conditions—those are lies where you can turn the tables.

FISH FAMILIAR WATER
When water is high and visibility is nil, stick to familiar streams and rivers where you already know the locations of trout and the details of various

runs. On unfamiliar water, you're fishing blind. You don't know whether a riffle is shallow and fishless or whether it's 3 feet deep with some productive pockets. You don't know whether the deepest slot in a run is near the center or along the bank. You can't see fly-eating logs lying on the bottom. But when you know which runs hold concentrations of trout and where trout are likely to hunker down within those runs, you can prospect the best refuge water methodically—and that's exactly what it takes to be successful in dirty water.

So take advantage of what you already know. After a storm, I often select some stream that's been frustrating me at low, clear flows—the kind of stream where just poking my head over the bank spooks one trout that races upstream, scattering several more. During a spate, all of the trout in a given run are likely to crowd into the most protected pocket. Suddenly marching right up to the fish is no problem. All I have to do is probe for that refuge pocket. And when I find it, there are plenty of eyeballs to detect my fly.

TRANSITION TIME

Following storms, most moving water drops faster than it clears. Often water levels return to near normal within a day, but silt takes a few days to settle out. Once high water abates, trout eventually leave refuge pockets to resume feeding on their normal stations. That transition usually occurs as visibility improves to several feet and trout can see well enough to feed efficiently.

As trout disperse from deep slots to scattered feeding stations, adjust your tactics. Scale down to a dark, midsize nymph or streamer that can be readily seen by trout and delivered accurately. During transition time, I combine short-line and long-line nymphing techniques. Trout that are holding on the bottom in 5 feet of water still can't see me, so I stand close to deep runs and nymph them with a short line. And I cover shallow feeding stations with longer casts. That involves constantly altering my split-shot arrangement to cover lies at various depths and current speeds, but it's usually worth the effort.

The final stages of clearing make for wonderful prospecting. In fact, it would be tough to design a better setup. Trout are feeding aggressively and unselectively to make up for missed meals, and there's still enough color in the water to camouflage you and your casting motions. Even if afternoon water temperatures climb to marginal readings, say 68 degrees, the action often remains surprisingly steady during transition.

AFTER THE GREAT FLOOD

Regions that receive substantial snow experience annual spring flooding. Snow thaws faster than the underlying earth, so absorption is minimal and most snowmelt runs directly into streams. That's why they call the season "runoff" in the mountainous West, where heavy snowpack and sudden warming unleash torrents.

When flows surge many times above normal, rivers and streams get facelifts whether they need them or not. Banks are washed out, logs and boulders are tossed around like Tinkertoys, and channels are rerouted. Powerful currents scour riverbeds and carry sediment downstream. Some dandy runs are blown out or filled in. Some new runs are gouged. Some trout go looking for new homes. Anglers need to explore once-familiar streams all over again to discover those new haunts.

That's exactly what happened in southwestern Wisconsin in the summer of 2000. I'm forty-six, and it was the most extreme flooding to hit Coulee Region trout streams in my lifetime. After a dry spring, late May was wet. The ground was already saturated when massive thunderstorms struck in early June. Narrow valleys were hammered with 10 inches of rain in a few hours, and there was nowhere for water to go except downhill. Trout streams that normally run 10 to 20 feet wide ran wider than football fields. The scouring in upper watersheds was incredible. When the big tap in the sky was turned off, some streams that had snaked between lush earthen banks over silt and gravel bottoms ran over naked limestone rubble that extended well beyond the normal high-water mark.

It made for an interesting summer of fishing and exploring. On some familiar streams in Crawford and southern Vernon Counties, it was like fishing brand new water. Some major runs that had held several dozen trout were completely erased. Some trout were certainly lost, but most of the fish were simply redistributed. Shortly after the flood, a fisheries crew electroshocked one stream section on two consecutive days and found a complete turnover in the trout population—a clear indication that trout were in flux and seeking new homes. In general, I thought more trout moved downstream than up.

The torrential rains really recharged the groundwater. Streams ran relatively high and cool throughout July and August, and I had excellent hot-weather action. Likewise, following a winter of heavy snowpack in the West, spring flooding is severe, but then flows and fishing hold up well through summer.

We'll be seeing the impact of the summer 2000 flood for years to come. In the short term, it devastated many streambanks and erased expensive habitat improvements. But it also flushed years of accumulated sediments from upper watersheds, and that should improve spawning success. Many warm, mucky beaver ponds were cleansed, renewing entire stream sections. Some beaver dams were quickly rebuilt, but old abandoned dams were cleared, which will mean cooler summer flows and increased migration of trout throughout watersheds. I just wonder where the slob brown that busted me off in April wound up, because his old lair is history.

Chapter 10

Targeting
Carnivorous Trout

The very richest tailwaters and spring creeks are fundamentally different from the ordinary waters that most of us frequent. Because of their exceptional fertility and stable temperatures, these elite waters host prolific insect hatches for much of the year. Their trout grow large gorging on a continuous slurry of mostly small organisms, which they take both on and below the surface. The feeding habits of trout that live in these invertebrate factories change very little as they grow. And grow they do. On the best catch-and-release tailwaters, large trout of 2 to 4 pounds outnumber small fish.

On less fertile streams that are open to liberal trout harvest, that scenario is reversed. Most trout are under a foot in length. It's the rare trout—less than 1 percent of the population—that ever reaches 20 inches. Trout that make that quantum leap in body size do it by finding a way to survive intense fishing pressure and by changing their feeding habits as they mature. As they grow much beyond a pound, these trophy-bound trout begin to feed mainly subsurface, and they capitalize on their own size by targeting large baitfish and crayfish that the bulk of the trout population is too small to tap into. Trout that manage to survive for a few seasons in the meat-eating mode become 20-inch fish. The very rare trout that grows to 2 feet or more in length is probably a cannibal as well as a carnivore. A brute like that is big enough to dominate nearly everything it swims with, including other trout. Such fish may rise during exceptionally heavy hatches of small insects or when large insects, like *Hexagenia* mayflies or grasshoppers, are available. But they have a definite tendency to feed subsurface and to target crustaceans and baitfish. That's particularly true of browns, which are the only 4-pound wild trout in most local fisheries.

As a class, the spring-fed limestone streams of southwestern Wisconsin are the most alkaline in the Midwest. Yet even on these fertile spring creeks, most of the major caddis and mayfly hatches occur in a narrow two-month window from mid-April to mid-June. And even during a major hatch, it's rare to see a 20-inch trout dimpling the surface. Catching these trout by prospecting on top between hatches is really bucking the odds. And that's the case on the vast majority of trout waters.

GET DOWN

On most waters, the surest way to increase your take of large trout is to get your fly down to their level more often. I routinely prospect subsurface between hatches. And I often prospect subsurface during hatches. Say what? That's right—during hatches, conditions are usually right for big trout to be active, even though they're not patrolling the top. We'll discuss prospecting deep during hatches in more detail a bit later.

Hatch or no hatch, don't let anybody convince you that fly-fishing subsurface is second-class sport. In many respects, fishing subsurface is more demanding than fishing on top. To mention just a few reasons, casting a weighted fly with precision is more difficult than flicking a dry fly; combating three-dimensional subsurface drag is much more difficult than nullifying two-dimensional surface drag; detecting a subtle subsurface strike is more difficult than seeing an obvious rise; and locating unseen fish is more difficult than stalking risers.

Esthetically, fly-fishing subsurface doesn't necessarily take a backseat to fishing dry. When performed at a high level, probing with a streamer, short-line nymphing, and long-line nymphing are precise and enjoyable techniques that, along with excellent hatch-matching skills, make you a versatile angler. I look at those who fish dry even when conditions don't warrant it, and I wonder: What could be less engaging than approaching the water with a fixed mindset and being a one-dimensional angler?

BIG FLIES FOR BIG FISH?

The correlation between chucking big flies and catching big trout is more than casual. So why not prospect full-time with a gigantic Roadkill Special? Well, if you're strictly interested in trophy trout and you're on sizable water, that's actually pretty sound strategy. But in most fisheries, a 20-inch trout is a one-in-five-hundred fish, and if you toss a fly that intimidates everything but the biggest fish, it can be a long time between hookups. And on small streams, you sacrifice too much control with outsize flies.

For small streams with good fish densities, the most productive prospecting strategy is to select a nymph or streamer that's big enough to interest top-end trout yet small enough for precise presentations. That allows you to catch trout in a range of sizes and to deliver the fly to tight spots. Even big trout will readily strike a modest-size fly—if you get it down where they can see it and grab it without much effort. How small can you go in a prospecting fly and still have a legitimate shot at big fish? On most streamtypes, I can consistently move top-end trout by prospecting with a size 12 nymph in a substantial pattern, like a Fuzzy Hare's Ear or a Soft-Hackle Woolly Worm. If I drop to size 16 in those same patterns, my encounters with big trout drop sharply.

If you're specifically targeting big fish in relatively big water, then go right to a big fly. When fishing lower watersheds for big, predatory browns on warm spring days, that's a perfect situation to go with a big streamer that's highly visible and appeals to the carnivorous trout found in these waters. Another good time to go big is when mature browns start moving toward spawning waters in early fall. In fact, whenever conditions are right for the very biggest trout to be highly active is a good time to go big.

How big should a big-fish streamer be? Toss the biggest fly that you can control under the circumstances. With a 3-weight rod, a size 8 streamer might be the biggest you can cast with authority. With a 7-weight rod, a size 1/0 streamer might be controllable. I do most of my nymphing and dry-fly fishing with 4-weight rods, but I pack a heavier backup rod that allows me to deliver a big nymph or streamer into some wind. In the Midwest, that's usually a 5-weight rod; in the West or on lakes, it's a 6- or 7-weight rod.

Big flies seduce big fish because they represent a substantial mouthful and because they're highly visible. To a big trout, a big morsel is more visible and worth moving farther for. That allows you to cover a lot of water with relatively few casts and to consistently move aggressive fish. In fact, big trout, sizable water, and extremely low trout densities often go hand in hand, and the most practical way to approach such water is to hit it when trout are aggressive, and then cover as much water as you can with a big streamer. Hit each productive lie with a few well-placed casts and move on. Sure, pounding any given run could produce a big fish on the twentieth cast. But you're a lot more likely to have a banner day on big, aggressive trout by covering several dozen runs with a few casts each than by pounding a few runs.

FISH THE PRIME AREAS AT THE PRIME TIMES
Big trout are seasoned veterans that have roamed a given watershed for at least a half dozen annual cycles. They know where to find throngs of baitfish in spring, cool water in July, and spawning gravel in September. Anticipate the seasonal needs of mature fish, and target the appropriate stream sections.

Small trout often feed when conditions are marginal, but big trout are models of efficiency—that's how they got big. As such, they feed almost exclusively when conditions are optimal. And carnivorous trout that target large prey feed infrequently and for short duration. To consistently catch big trout, you have to haunt productive water at prime times. For much of the season, that means rising earlier or fishing later than the crowds.

FISH AT NIGHT

As summer advances and afternoon water temperatures soar to uncomfortable levels, some of the biggest trout prowl primarily under the cover of darkness, and night is prime time to hunt these lunkers.

Prospecting unfamiliar water at night is rarely productive and can be downright dangerous. Instead, target pools that you know hold a big fish or two and where you're familiar with the terrain and its hazards—hot fences, ornery bulls, beaver channels. A sound strategy is to canvass several lunker lairs in a vicinity on the same night. That increases your chances of bumping into a big fish on the prowl, and a single encounter is all it takes to make sleep deprivation worthwhile.

One drawback to fishing at night is that it leaves you groggy the next day. Most hard-core night anglers adjust to a nocturnal schedule by sleeping days. For anglers who don't have that luxury, a good alternative to fishing at night is to be on the water before daybreak, fish through the cool morning hours, and skip the late afternoon and evening session, when summer water temperatures are high anyway. Then turn in early, so you're ready to fish before sunup the next day. In summer, big trout are often aggressive at daybreak, and you can see well enough to fish unfamiliar waters or streams that are simply difficult to negotiate.

Night fishing gives you many of the same advantages that off-color water affords you. By walking and wading quietly, you can get close to your target water without being seen. That allows you to make short casts and stay out of trouble. Obviously, meadow streams are easier to fish in the dark than woodland streams. And provided that the wading isn't too hazardous, big streams and rivers are much easier to work than small streams, because you can use the open channel for unobstructed backcasting, and your casting doesn't need to be nearly as precise.

Just as in dirty water, go with big flies that trout can readily see. At night, big trout hunt by sound as much as sight, so noisy flies are great attractors. Once your eyes adjust to the dark, you can usually see an attack on a surface bug or a big dry fly and strike with authority.

Trout tend to hit noisy surface bugs on the first presentation or not at all, which makes them valuable indicator flies for determining how aggressive trout are. If you pull a topwater bug over a slick that you know holds big fish and you get no response, you'll probably need to probe methodically in deep refuge water to score on that particular night.

When big trout are active at night, they often leave refuge water to prowl shallows and slack water where baitfish school, so it's important to cover backwaters and stream margins. Fish are easily spooked out of shallows, so cover them first and then work the deep water.

Night fishing is a sort of netherworld where you hook bats on your backcasts, bump into foraging skunks and 60-pound beavers, and glimpse scorpions in your flashlight beam. It's an interesting change of pace that's highly stimulating to the senses, not to mention the imagination. And it's definitely a good time to target big trout when the heat is on during the day.

WORK NEGLECTED WATERS

The rare trout that survives to trophy size in a liberal-harvest stream isn't necessarily superwary. Some fish just live in neglected water.

Neglected water takes many forms. Brown trout that spend the spring foraging on baitfish in lower watersheds that aren't considered to be trout water see very few anglers during the peak fishing months, which greatly boosts their survival rate. Likewise, streams that snake through jungles of downed box elder or head-high nettles see little angling traffic in summer, and those are good streams to hit in early spring before the foliage erupts.

Some of my favorite big-fish streams are marginal trout water with successful but limited natural reproduction. They supported more trout at one time, but they've been badly silted by poor land-use practices. As their reputations have declined, people have simply quit fishing them. Now hordes of chubs and shiners peck incessantly at my flies and strike indicators, as the trout are too scarce to hold baitfish numbers in check. But the scattered trout that are around gorge on baitfish in isolation and have a good shot at surviving for several years. These streams are good bets to produce a 3-pound or better trout if I hit them when conditions are prime and I cover a lot of water.

Your chance of catching an exceptional trout on public water often increases in direct proportion to your distance from a road. I spent nearly twenty summers fishing out of a backpack, so I know something about chasing trout that live way off the beaten path. (If you're intrigued by this approach, see my first book, *Fly-Fishing the Rocky Mountain Backcountry*.) But relatively neglected water exists even in farm country. Keep an eye open for streams that swing away from roads for a mile or more or have roadless headwaters. Nine out of ten anglers stick to roadside waters that are easy to fish. And even the popular catch-and-release rivers usually have some out-of-the-way stretches.

Anglers who are ambitious enough to walk 5 to 10 miles a day bump into more than their share of trophy trout, including some that are very catchable. When you do locate a big trout in an isolated spot, there's a good chance it will be there and unmolested for some time. Even if you don't land it on your initial encounter, you may well succeed on a repeat visit. That scenario produced my biggest Wisconsin trout of last season—a mean-mawed, 25-inch brown that I took on a small spring creek that holds mostly brook trout. The brown busted me off on a 4X tippet in April. I didn't return until Father's Day, but as I eased into casting range, I spotted it right where I'd hooked it before. On the first cast, it took my Soft-Hackle Woolly Worm—the same fly it had taken in April. This time I was equipped with a fresh 3X tippet and was able to put the skids to the fish every time it made for its lair under a big boulder.

Landing a wild brown like that on a local creek, especially on a liberal-harvest creek where a trout must beat tremendous odds to attain that size, is the kind of angling thrill that can't be bought. For sheer satisfaction, I rank that brown right up there with the rampaging 25-inch golden trout that I took on the roof of Wyoming's Wind River Range after hiking over a thousand miles in pursuit of trophy goldens.

WORK DIFFICULT LIES

Trout that grow old in heavily fished liberal-harvest streams have something special going for them, and that something is often a difficult lie.

On some runs, it's nearly impossible to slip into casting position without being detected, especially when many sets of eyes are watching. On one of my local streams, an exceptionally long run is packed with dozens of trout in various sizes, including a few 3- to 4-pound browns that spend most of their time clustered on the bottom in the middle of the run. In a half dozen visits, I've taken just one big fish. Getting a fly down on the bottom in the center of the run without hooking or riling smaller trout is no small feat. In effect, the small fish act as sentinels for the big ones, and it's difficult to slip past dozens of sentinels.

Many anglers believe that an absence of baitfish or small trout in a run suggests that a big, predatory trout is present, but that's rarely true. Carnivorous trout, by their very nature, settle into substantial pools and runs that attract slews of small trout and baitfish. Prey fish scatter when predators are in the attack mode, but then they quickly settle back into prime real estate, they don't abandon it. During periods of inactivity, I frequently see chubs and small trout lying belly-to-belly with browns that are big enough to inhale them.

Speaking of difficult lies, when carnivorous trout are hungry, they often station near the tails of runs because that puts prey fish out front where they can be eyeballed for any sign of vulnerability and then exploded upon. At prime feeding times, always work or observe tails carefully before approaching, or you'll wind up flushing some big fish. When you cast directly upstream into the tail of a run, the tailout current snatches your line and quickly drags your fly downstream. If you locate a big brown that likes to feed in a tail, try him in low light or off-color water, when you can get close and fish with almost no line on the water. In broad daylight, I often work tails by kneeling well back from the water and casting at a sharp angle to the streambed. Even if I have to drape my fly line over land to remain out of sight, I can usually get at least one clean drift through a tail before the fly or the line fouls.

Many big trout survive intense fishing pressure by hanging out where they can break you off in a heartbeat. I had a supercharged encounter with a brown like that this spring on a small Wisconsin stream. He was dwelling under a toppled tree in a tangle of exposed roots. The pool couldn't be worked from below, so I walked right up to the head, using a big stump for cover, and dropped a weighted Bi-Bugger off the 4-foot-high bank. A monster brown shot out of the tangle and snatched the fly off the bottom right at my feet. Even with 3X tippet, I knew it would be a very brief ride. The fish had to scoot only a yard to bury itself in cover. I was left with my leader butt and several feet of fly line spaghettied through the root system. As I poked and prodded with the rod tip, trying to extricate the line, I had smaller trout zipping all over. Then I heard a tremendous thrashing and looked up to see the boss vacating the pool. As he bolted through the shallow tailout, his massive back was completely exposed, and he churned silt and threw water like a half-beached salmon. I dropped my 4-weight rod

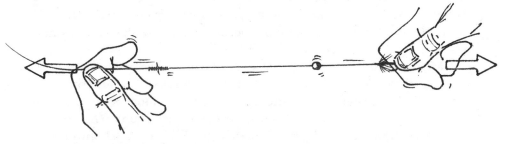

Grasp the hook by the bend and the tippet above the splicing knot and pull in opposite directions so that you can feel the tippet stretching or "bouncing."

and sprinted after him. I was right on his tail as he scooted through a long shallows—and he was easily on the high side of 25 inches.

I made plans to go back at him with the same fly and presentation, using 0X tippet, which I would have used the first time, and probably gotten away with, if I'd known he was there. Before I got the opportunity, a massive June flood blew out the pool. I haven't relocated him, but that's right up there on my to-do list.

BEEF UP YOUR RIGGING AND MAINTAIN IT CAREFULLY

Big trout are rarely hooked on tackle that allows you to overpower them. But you tip the odds in your favor by using the biggest hooks and heaviest tippets you can get away with under the circumstances. A slight increase in the size of either component can make all the difference when something outsize grabs your fly.

Rather than defeating drag by reducing tippet diameter, try increasing tippet length to 3 feet or more. A 3-foot, 3X tippet is nearly as flexible and fast-sinking as a 2-foot, 4X tippet. And longer tippets absorb more shock, which effectively increases their breaking strength. I rarely prospect with anything under 4X, and in recent years I'm going more and more to 3X or even 2X for size 8 to 12 nymphs and streamers, especially on small streams, where big fish have to be kept on a short leash or kissed good-bye. By and large, most trout anglers fish a little lighter tippet than they really need to. And, as I've learned painfully over the years, when you routinely rig on the light side, there's a good chance that the really big fish are going to clean your clock.

Check your tippet frequently. Feel for nicks and fraying. After pinching on a split shot, slide it a short distance and check to make sure you haven't crimped the line. Use the bounce test to quickly check the integrity of your hook knot, tippet, and tippet knot. Pinch the hook securely in one hand, grab the leader just above the tippet knot with the other hand, and make a quick pull, exerting enough pressure to stretch or bounce the tippet. Occasionally, something will fail with alarming ease right in your hands, which is where you want it to happen.

LOOK ALIVE OUT THERE

There are more ways to bust off big trout than I care to document here. But I've certainly felt my share of tight lines go suddenly and sickeningly slack.

On Depuy's Spring Creek, I had a huge rainbow that was starting to tire exit a pond by swimming downstream through a culvert. I didn't expect it to do that, or I would have moved well away from the culvert as I gained line.

On the upper Missouri, I was spooled by a tremendous brown that stripped my entire fly line plus 100 yards of backing in one sizzling run. I was wading below an island that shelved into deep water, so I couldn't follow. When I was down to nothing but black-anodized arbor, the fish was considerate enough to give me a parting glance by tail-walking across the surface. Even at 130 yards, he looked stunning—maybe 10 pounds. In that situation, with 4X, I had no chance to stop him.

On the San Juan, I was a tad slow in releasing the line from against the rod grip after a hook set—it was a frosty September sunup and my digits were numb. Instantaneously, the rod tip snapped downward with ferocious force, and the line recoiled like a broken rubber band. Thirty yards downstream, something silver and of remarkable girth vaulted into the air and hit the water with a resounding thwack. I'm still not sure if that was a rainbow trout or a runaway jet ski from Navajo Reservoir.

On the Madison River, I lost an alligator-size brown that I really earned, and he was all but mine when I muffed him. This was in the mid-1980s, when the Madison was fishing phenomenally. I'd been on the river for nearly two weeks and had landed dozens of hot fish, when I saw a head-to-tail rise that was head and shoulders above anything I've ever seen on the Madison. It was close to dark, and the fish didn't rise again. I searched the slick with attractor drys, nymphs, and Buggers on 3X tippets—stuff I thought I had a prayer to handle him on—but no banana.

The next evening I was back on that slick with my eyeballs peeled. A half hour before dark, he rolled again—twice. He spurned fly after fly as I stepped my way down in hook size and tippet. It was getting dark when I switched to a size 16 Rusty Spinner on 5X—a fly I've always done well with on the Madison at last light. On the first drift, he took with the slow-motion roll of a really big riser. My strike felt rock solid, but the hook came free. Well, at least I'd tweaked him.

Evening three found me right back there. Once again, the fish moved into the slick shortly before dark. That evening, he was more active. I saw him rise a half dozen times in a half hour, always on the same seam about 10 feet below a big boulder that deflected heavy current. By now I'd seen him well enough that I was sure he'd tape on the obscene side of 27 inches. I locked in on that seam with the same size 16 Rusty Spinner he'd taken the previous evening, and he eventually took it again. On the Madison, I've had loads of hot trout go cartwheeling downstream, but this fish shot into the powerful main flow and bored straight upriver along the bottom. As my entire fly line bellied and strummed like a guitar string in the current, he sulked down there. At times I thought I was fouled and that he was gone, but then I'd feel him shaking his head. I expected it to be the tippet that parted. But when the line finally went limp and I cranked in, I still had my fly. The hook had snapped at the top of the bend.

Evening four finds me back for more abuse—I really want this brown. I bump my rig up to 4X and a size 14 Rusty Spinner. Just before it's too dark to make out riseforms, I hook him again. He does the upstream thing, boring along the bottom until he's almost into my backing, and then hunkering down in some kind of refuge pocket he has out there. He's immovable. All I can do is apply as much pressure as I dare and hope that it's enough to faze him. After five minutes, the line goes abruptly limp and my heart swoons, but after a few panicky cranks, the line tightens again. Apparently he's slipped downstream a few yards before digging back in. Then he slips downstream like that with abrupt little jolts, giving bits of ground at shorter and shorter intervals. Suddenly he abandons the upstream fight altogether and heads for Ennis. It's off to the races, with me running in the dark over greased cannonballs to prevent being spooled. I've popped off my share of 3-pound Madison River trout that pulled this stunt; with this bruiser, I really have my hands full. He takes me down, down, down, a couple hundred yards and well into my backing. Somewhere in there I scramble over a split-rail cattle fence that extends a few feet into the river, but that part of the battle is all a blur—just churning thighs and visceral grunts as my knees and ankles are wrenched every which way, until he finally stops and I quickly recover the backing and most of the line. I'm incredulous that my 4X hasn't vaporized, and I'm swearing lifelong allegiance to Dai-Riki.

At last I'm able to apply the rod butt and steer him into a quiet side slick, where I have him contained on little more than the leader. It's inky black now. I can't see him 5 feet away. He circles me slowly, ominously. When he turns on his side, I should be able to see him and use the net. But after five minutes on a short line, he's still ebony side up. Any mortal trout would have turned over by now, but I haven't seen so much as a tail or caudal fin break the surface. He must be as thick as he is long. I begin to doubt the capacity of my net and whether I can dip it deftly enough in the dark.

There's a gentle gravel bar handy, so I consider beaching him. I bring him around for a practice pass, and he feels controllable. As I bring him to the bar again, he makes a little spurt. No problem—I'll just bring him around again. Except that when he makes that spurt, my feet are spread, and he scoots between my legs. The tippet grabs a speed hook on my wading boot. Ping.

For the next eighteen months, I was not myself. And I don't say that completely in jest. I recently read again that too many fly fishers take the sport too seriously, and how that's a misguided approach—that it's all too much good, clean, inconsequential fun to be taken seriously. Well, when botching a Madison River brown of that size doesn't deflate me like a mule kick to the gut, I'll know I've lost any vital enthusiasm for rivers and much of my capacity to have fun with a fly rod.

Fortunately, I've landed a few I shouldn't have. My biggest golden trout was snatched from the jaws of impending defeat. I was dead drifting a scud on 4X in a swift, deep outlet flow when I hooked him. He headed out into the lake on a scorching run that included a half dozen jumps. En route, he went around the far side of a big, exposed boulder, threading my line beneath it. The line grabbed and grated as it peeled out. The outlet was too deep to cross, so I instinctively did what turned out to be the right thing—I ran downstream away from the fish. Doing that decreased the angle of the line around the rock and generated enough slack that I was able to roll-cast up and over the boulder and get tight to the fish. He was a golden to knock your eyes out—as radiant as they come, and right on 25 inches with tremendous girth. That particular lake is 30 rugged miles from the trailhead, and that was my third trip in, so I had some serious sweat equity invested. And I'd made dozens of solo treks over the past decade to other golden lakes scattered across the roof of the Rockies. To finally land a golden of that caliber was fun—serious fun.

The fighting abilities of trout are underappreciated by the general angling populace. That's understandable, because most bass fishermen, for instance, have never caught a good trout on a fly or pursued big trout in a brawling river like the Madison, where the fish are jet propelled. Here in the upper Midwest, where we have an abundance of big smallmouth bass, I often hear the claim that smallies fight harder than trout. Smallies are fine fly-rod quarry, and I enjoy canoeing their beautiful north-country waters, but I've lipped dozens of 4-pound smallmouths, and I can't recall one that ran into my backing, even when I was throwing 70 feet of fly line. Granted, I'm usually rigged with 0X, but I fish smallies on my trout reels, and under just the click resistance of the drag they don't run far. I've had plenty of 4-pound trout hooked right off my rod tip, in both lakes and rivers, run into my backing lickety-split under identical click tension. In the stamina department, smallies use their slab bodies to generate tremendous leverage in the short term, but big trout take much longer to tire, even when you're rigged heavy enough to apply significant pressure from the get-go. In the jumping category, smallies do shatter the surface and throw enough spray into a canoe that I've thought about installing windshield wipers on my Costa Del Mars, but I've had 4-pound rainbows rocket above my hat brim when I was wading knee-deep. Bottom line: Trout of equal size run farther and faster, last longer, and can jump higher. At the top of their game, trout are more athletic.

As for suspense, other freshwater fish are routinely hooked on heavy enough tackle that when they pull, you just pull right back. And big smallmouths, walleyes, muskies, whatever, are usually caught from boats in relatively big, slow water, where they're easily followed and steered clear of trouble. A big trout hooked on a gossamer tippet in a fast, rocky river goes pretty much where it wants at the opening bell. It uses the current to amplify its strength, and as a shallow-water fish, it has a nose for cover—it will try to use boulders, undercut banks, stumps, or logs to short-circuit a fight in the opening seconds. And trout rivers are nasty turf, where it's tough for a wading angler to follow quickly enough to gain or maintain an advantage. Landing a big trout on typical fly tackle in moving water is a touch-and-go, thrust-and-parry affair that taxes your tippet, your touch, your cool, your sense of anticipation, and your fish-fighting technique. Line and rod angles change abruptly as a fish repositions. It's always a fine line between letting the fish dictate the fight and applying too much pressure for one costly instant. Every veteran of the trout wars can look back on dream fish that escaped by brute force, bad fortune, or some silly miscue. With experience, you start to win more of those battles, but big trout can humble anyone.

When you do mange to maneuver a big trout onto a short leash, look alive out there and have a plan for landing him. On long hikes and brushy streams, I rarely carry a net, but I always keep a bandanna or light glove handy for tailing. Cloth provides traction as you grab a fish by the tail shank—the one place you can squeeze a trout without damaging internal organs. If you use a net, examine the bag periodically—yes, I've had trout swim right through my net.

And, oh yeah, keep your legs together.

IGNORING A HATCH

This may strike dry-fly enthusiasts as heresy, but during many hatches on many waters, you can catch bigger trout by ignoring the hatch and probing deep with a sizable nymph or streamer. Insect hatches usually coincide with very favorable feeding temperatures, so big trout are usually aggressive during hatches, even if they're not rising. That makes hatches one of the best times to target them.

Yeah, but at the expense of riveting dry-fly action? Here's how I look at it: There are many days when I can catch average trout on top, but there are a very limited number of days when big trout are highly active in daylight. By devoting some hatch hours to targeting big trout subsurface, I significantly increase my encounters with top-end fish. And over the course of a season, I still catch plenty of trout on drys.

Sometimes ignoring a hatch means heading for neglected water. For instance, spring afternoons in Wisconsin often produce excellent mayfly or caddis hatches in high-quality habitats that support slews of 9- to 13-inch trout. During hatches, you can run up fantastic numbers of fish on dry flies. It's common to see a dozen trout puckering a pool the size of a double bed, and there can be a half dozen pools like that in a quarter-mile stretch. By the end of a brisk three-hour hatch, you have a mating cluster of battered drys in your fly patch, and you can't even begin to recall all of the solid foot-long fish you've released. Yet on days like that, I often wind up fishing downstream in fairly degraded habitat where hatches are light or absent. Why? Because those spring days are also tops for targeting trout of 17 inches and up with big flies in lower watersheds. Experience has taught me that by chasing hatches in this region, I'm targeting the smallest 95 percent of the trout population. By ignoring some of those hatches, I'm able to target the largest 5 percent of the trout when they're very aggressive. It's an approach that can be applied in most regions.

Making the call on where and how to fish is always subjective. It boils down to knowing the nature of your local waters, and then playing the percentages according to what intrigues you at the time—action or size. It's really no different on hatch days.

Of course, trout aren't always segregated by size, and big trout don't live strictly in low-density waters. Many stream sections are heavily salted with small trout and peppered with a large fish or two. So what kind of presentation will move those better fish during hatches? Well, if you're seeing good snouts, there's no reason not to go right at them with a dry. But during many hatches, especially caddis hatches, you'll often catch more trout, period, by working an appropriate emerger imitation subsurface. Sometimes getting your emerger down just a bit puts it at the level of good fish that aren't working the top, and they grab it. But often, by ignoring the prevailing hatch and prospecting deep with a sizable nymph or streamer, you'll move big trout more quickly and consistently.

I bumped into a classic example of that last April during a heavy hatch of grannom caddis. As I approached a run where I'd taken nice fish before, nothing was rising, but I eventually spotted the flashing of a good trout taking emergers deep. I put my pupal imitation right in its lane more than a dozen times, but my fly was ignored, even though the continual flashing in the depths indicated that the fish was feeding very energetically. So I threw a change-up—a Soft-Hackle Woolly Worm that was bigger and darker than the naturals. On the very first drift, I hooked what turned out to be a 17-inch rainbow that had a gut for the Guinness Book.

Its belly was grotesquely distended. For its size, the rainbow surrendered meekly, and no wonder—it could barely swim without bursting. As I led the trout into a quiet eddy, it disgorged a thick chum, and as I gently supported the fish, it backfired again, spewing countless caddis pupae—hundreds and hundreds of identical little victims ingested in a selective feeding frenzy. And yet the trout had grabbed my Woolly Worm on the first drift, but it had refused my pupal imitation repeatedly. Why? Well, maybe my pupal imitation wasn't refused but simply overlooked as the trout gorged on throngs of naturals. Eventually the trout may have selected my emerger. But the Woolly was taken on the very first drift, probably because it was easily differentiated. I've had this kind of experience so many times that I've come to expect it.

And think about this common scenario: What if that same rainbow is working caddis emergers too deeply for me to see it? Now I don't know where the fish is, or even that it's there. Even when I knew its precise location, a dozen presentations weren't sufficient. What are my chances of taking that specific fish with a small emerger by blindly probing the entire run? With a dozen casts, not very good. Maybe with several dozen casts the rainbow will see and eventually take my fly. But with a bigger prospecting nymph, I know my fly will be noticed quickly.

OK, but what about selectivity? Well, selectivity didn't keep that rainbow from whacking a size 12 Woolly Worm when it was more pumped up from feeding selectively on size 16 emerging caddis than any trout I've ever seen. The best predictor of how selective big fish will be during a hatch is to consider the nature of the fishery. If big fish routinely feed on prolific hatches, expect them to be selective. But if big fish are primarily carnivorous and opportunistic, they'll probably grab a sizable nymph even during the odd times when they're grazing on hatches. The bulk of their experience has groomed them to grab a substantial mouthful.

Now imagine that there are six big, carnivorous brown trout scattered throughout two dozen runs in a mile-long meadow. A caddis hatch is in progress and many small trout are working on top, but all six of the good fish are working emergers too deeply to be spotted by an angler. Joe and Moe pull up to the stream in Joe's spanking new SUV with OH2-FSH vanity plates. The stage is set for some great fishing, but Joe is in a tizzy. He announces that they must split for home in an hour so he can wash and vacuum his vehicle. (He hadn't realized they were going to be driving on gravel.) Anyway, Joe spends the hour hovering near the truck and methodically probing just three runs with the appropriate caddis drys and emergers. Moe runs and guns the entire meadow, firing a few casts in each run with a big prospecting nymph fished deep. One of them catches two 17-inch browns and a dandy 19-incher. Which one? Well, Moe is the only one who gave himself a shot to do it.

STRADDLING THE FENCE

I often take a split approach during hatches. If I see rising fish, I go at them with a dry or an emerger and have some surface fun. But before leaving the run, I switch to a bigger nymph and prospect deep, especially if I'm only seeing small snouts and I know that a stream holds good fish. What happens? Every spring I get some of my biggest browns while prospecting deep during hatches. And even when I don't hook anything particularly large, I usually take some respectable trout that aren't rising. In fact, on average, the trout I catch by prospecting deep are a good 2 to 3 inches longer and significantly heftier than those I catch by matching the hatch. It's an approach worth employing wherever top-end trout don't rise habitually—in other words, on most waters. Give it a legitimate go on your local waters, and you may discover that during hatches you've just been skimming the surface.

If you're changing from a nymph to a dry and back again several times during a hatch, you should streamline the process. If I'm fishing a dry on a 5X tippet and I decide to switch to a nymph, I clip the entire tippet with the dry still attached so I can get back to the dry quickly. With the 5X removed, I tie the nymph directly to the exposed 4X segment of the leader, keeping the 4X segment about 18 inches long so that it functions as a viable tippet. Putty strike indicators are the ticket, because they're reusable and can be repositioned quickly. To switch back to the dry, all I have to do is clip the nymph, strip off the split shot and indicator, and reattach the prerigged 5X tippet.

Fishing a dry fly with a nymph dropper is another approach, though, if you run a sizable prospecting nymph under a small hatch-matching dry, the dry will be pulled under. I'm not big on two-fly combinations. From executing a difficult cast to achieving a long drag-free drift, I can fish a solo dry or nymph more precisely.

Chapter 11

Probing
Lunker Structures

Roughly twenty-five thousand years ago, the last major glaciation leveled the Midwest but spared the Driftless Area—a rolling upland that covers the southwestern quarter of Wisconsin. Over time, hundreds of spring-fed streams carved this limestone-rich upland into a maze of ridges and narrow coulees. Today dozens of fertile valley streams harbor strong populations of wild brown trout. On the better streams, action for adult browns of 12 to 14 inches is superb, even when measured against famed eastern and Rocky Mountain waters. And there are enough 20-inch-plus browns swimming around to keep things interesting. Native brook trout still dominate some headwaters and are reclaiming some of their former range; I'm catching brookies of a foot and longer in an increasing number of meadow sections that were brown trout strongholds just a few years ago. And there are scattered wild rainbows. Hatchery rainbows and browns are still being stocked to provide put-and-take fishing in a few streams, but the trend is toward transferring wild fish to help establish wild trout populations where habitat has been improved.

Fortunately, Wisconsin has extremely liberal stream access laws: You can legally wade any stream as long as you stay below the regular high-water mark and don't reach the stream by crossing private property without permission. Most landowners allow angling anyway, and the state purchases long-term public-fishing easements where trout-stamp funds are spent to improve habitat. The excellent access gives every angler a stake in seeing the fishing continue to improve throughout the region. Just twenty years ago, most area anglers fished bait or hardware, toted canvas creels, and killed their best trout. (I grew up fishing here with an 8-foot Shakespeare Wonder Rod Fly Rod and chub tails.) But today most dedicated trout anglers are fly fishers who routinely practice catch and release, even on streams that are open to harvest. The word is getting out about the fishing—the area is sometimes hyped as "the Montana of the Midwest"—and I regularly see vehicles from Illinois, Minnesota, Michigan, Iowa, and even Missouri parked along the well-known special-regulation streams. But what keeps me enthused, after four-plus decades of prowling the Coulee Region, are the many unheralded spring creeks that are fascinating to explore. Anyone who puts forth the effort will find fine fishing and a degree of solitude that's all but vanished from public trout water in populated regions. (Milwaukee, Minneapolis, and Chicago are all within a three- to four-hour drive.)

Southwestern Wisconsin is dairy country. More than a century of plowing and grazing the hilly terrain has silted and warmed many streams, especially in their lower reaches, where gradient decreases. Some streams are still being severely damaged by poor farming practices. Other streams are threatened by residential or industrial development, including large-scale hog and dairy operations. But in some drainages, shifting land-use patterns, including an increase in Conservation Reserve Program acreage and the conversion of marginal farmland to recreational ownership, have reduced erosion while increasing groundwater absorption. Springs that haven't flowed for decades are reemerging. As flows and temperatures improve, populations of scuds, sculpins, and insects are increasing, and trout are rebounding on their own in some streams. A few of my favorite streams have not received a dime for habitat improvement and are not protected by no-kill or slot-size regulations.

But many of the healthiest streams with the highest trout densities have benefited from extensive habitat restoration. On model streams, such as Timber Coulee and the West Fork of the Kickapoo River, habitat has been improved so dramatically that put-and-take fisheries have been converted to self-sustaining fisheries that harbor more than a thousand wild trout per mile. The pace of stream restoration has accelerated in the last decade, thanks to a few ambitious state fishing managers and some active fishing clubs, including Trout Unlimited and Federation of Fly Fishers chapters. Funds from a state trout stamp are channeled into stream improvement, and fishing organizations provide additional money and manpower.

In a typical restoration project, eroding streambanks are stabilized with rock riprap. Spill ramps, current deflectors, and boulders are installed to increase oxygenation and scouring, which helps flush sediment. Lunker structures—specialized wooden fish cribs—are tied directly into streambanks with steel rods and heavy rock. When combined with rock riprap, lunker structures stabilize streambanks and withstand all but the most severe flooding very well. Developed by the Wisconsin Department of Natural Resources, lunkers are now in use throughout the Midwest and are common in western Wisconsin.

Lunker Structures act as artificial cutbanks, greatly increasing the amount of secure refuge cover on small streams.

Basically, lunker structures are artificial cutbanks that provide trout with shade and overhead protection from predators, including herons, which can exact a heavy toll of trout on small streams. A dozen lunker structures scattered over a mile can easily increase the amount of secure refuge cover on a small creek by several hundred percent. With the installation of lunker structures on streams with good fertility, along with no-kill or restricted-harvest regulations, trout numbers usually jump dramatically. Habitat projects tend to generate increased angling pressure, at least in the short term, but as more and more stream mileage is improved, pressure is dispersed. Now, even on weekends, I often find myself fishing alone on out-of-the way streams that have received considerable habitat work.

READING LUNKER STRUCTURES

A lunker structure is an open-framed wooden crib that measures about 8 feet long by 3 feet wide by 1 foot high. Typically, a structure is placed where a riffle piles against an outside bend and deepens into a run. Two or more structures can be linked to form a long undercut. Structures are covered with riprap or with dirt and seeded. On a shallow run, trout seek refuge inside the open-framed crib. On a deep run, trout are able to tuck back under the bank a good 3 feet and completely under the structure.

A single lunker structure may be placed in a section of riprap that's many yards long. As you approach an unfamiliar run, look for big rocks right down on the waterline. Those rocks are used to anchor the structure, and they reveal its precise location. Some structures jut a bit into the current on their upstream end and are easily identified.

When trout are active, they disperse throughout a run. You'll see trout feeding in open riffles and tailouts and in the center of runs, just as they do in runs without structures. Many trout establish feeding stations on the outside edges of structures, where they're protected by the overhead bank yet can see food drifting on the open stream surface. Often, getting such fish to rise requires a very precise presentation, with the fly riding within an inch or two off the bank.

When they're inactive, trout often tuck well back under structures. While these fish can be tough to get a fly into, at least you know precisely where they are. And with a little practice, you'll become adept at drifting nymphs and streamers well back under structures.

You don't have to go for broke on the first presentation. In fact, by making your first cast right to the upstream end of a structure, you risk lining fish that are holding near the downstream end or in open water. As you approach a run, make your initial casts to the tailout and to the center to see if there are active fish out in the run. Then cast tight to the lower end of the structure. Finally, cast to the upstream end of the structure. Continue to work the structure until you achieve a full-length drift, with the fly swinging well back under the bank—that's where most fish will be, especially the good ones.

It's tough to get a drift well back under a structure while you're standing on top of it. Also, if you walk on the structure, there's a good chance that fish will see you or detect vibrations. So I usually work structures by wading in the stream or from the opposite bank. The opposite bank is usually the low, shallow bank, and from there I can kneel to stay under the sight line of fish. Every structure is laid out a bit differently, so it often takes several casts, and a series of adjustments, to get the fly to suck back under the structure on a nice dead drift. Conflicting currents or eddies in the middle of a pool or run can grab the line and drag the fly into open water. If you're casting to a structure along the far bank and you're being defeated by current in the center of the run, try casting backhanded over your off shoulder; that completely changes the angle of the rod, allowing you to lay the line parallel and very tight to the bank, in a way that can be difficult to achieve even with a reach cast. Various slack-line casts will also extend your drifts.

KEEPING BIG FISH OUT OF THE WOODWORK

Working from the bank opposite the structure gives you some leverage if you hook a good fish. Big browns invariably try to power back under the structure, and they can get there in a hurry. If you're standing on top of the structure, a big fish can scoot back under your feet, and you're at a lousy angle to prevent that from happening. From the bank opposite the structure, you can drop the rod low to angle the line safely under the outside edge of the structure and pressure the fish toward the center of the stream. By quickly moving upstream until you're even with the fish, you shorten the line and gain a better angle for forcing the fish out from under the bank.

Go ahead and test your tippet to the breaking point right from the get-go, because if a big fish buries back under a structure, it will bust you off anyway. Once you do force a good fish into open water, apply heavy pressure from the rod butt as soon as you sense the fish gathering steam for another run under the structure. To keep a big trout on a very short line without popping a 3X or 4X tippet, you have to milk every bit of shock-absorbency out of the rod. That means pointing the butt cap right at the fish and forcing the rod to bend all the way into the grip.

STRUCTURE STRATEGY
When a stream is targeted for extensive habitat improvement, fishing pressure often escalates right along with the trout population. But even if it's loaded with trout and managed under no-kill regulations, a small stream is still a small stream. You can't run an angler up its banks every fifteen minutes without putting the fish down. On weekends, when it's often impossible to get a crack at undisturbed water, you're better off fishing elsewhere. The good news is that a single well-publicized, special-regulation stream can siphon off the lion's share of fishing pressure from surrounding streams. I'm always amazed at how the majority of anglers stick to a few officially anointed waters, even when catch rates are dismal compared to lightly fished streams within a few miles.

As crowds flock to a rehabilitated stream, trout become skittish, and you need to adjust your prospecting tactics accordingly. Attractor flies quickly lose their effectiveness as fish become accustomed to inspecting potential food carefully. Generally, you want to drop down in fly size and closely imitate the prevailing food forms, even when prospecting. Since trout densities are high, you don't have to worry about a small fly being overlooked. Just strive to make your presentations look natural.

Too much of a good thing, including habitat improvement, can be bad. In recent years, I've watched trout numbers climb so high on one intensively rehabilitated stream that growth rates have tailed off. Baitfish populations have been depleted, and low numbers of robust trout have been replaced by pods of comparatively skinny trout. The stream is widely hailed as a success story and anglers flock to it, but to me the good old days were a decade ago, before the habitat was improved a lick and I could run and gun 3 miles of stream in a morning without seeing anyone—and I'd take more 3-pound trout in a weekend than I could take there now in an entire season. Don't get me wrong; there are a lot more fish now, and there are still some good fish around, but the nature of the fishing has changed.

The type of habitat improvement that I really keep an eye peeled for is small-scale stuff on out-of-the-way streams. I salivated two summers back when I saw an isolated series of lunker structures being installed in a cow pasture in a badly silted lower watershed where trout densities were so low that few people fished. I knew that mature browns dropping downstream to winter would probably discover the new shelters and set up shop. I hit those structures during a soft April shower, when trout metabolisms were racing and the water was off-color, so I could stand close to the structures and work a bugger drag-free on a short line. For an hour or so, it was like being in Montana. I took only a half dozen browns from the dozen or so structures. But they were all deep-bodied specimens of 16 to 20 inches. The lunker structures that are farthest downstream on any given stream definitely bear watching, because they tend to attract big browns as they drop downstream to winter and again as they move upstream in summer.

Several years ago, lunker structures were installed on a tiny step-across headwater creek that's too small and overgrown to fly-fish, even where it's deep enough to hold trout. I thought it was sort of questionable to invest time and money in rehabilitating water that was too small to fish, and indeed, I've never seen anyone fishing there. But a mile below the structures, where the stream gathers additional springs and grows a bit, there's an overgrazed cow pasture that has been retired to CRP for a few years now. That meadow is rejuvenating itself. Much of the accumulated silt has been flushed away, and the amount of chest-deep refuge water has increased tenfold in the last few years. Nobody messes with that little, out-of-the-way meadow either, even though the creek is fishable at that point and is suddenly home to a surprising number of browns in the 16-inch class. While those tiny lunker structures upstream didn't provide additional fishing, they clearly raised spawning success to a new level. And few who look at those little structures guess at the impact they've had just downstream.

Anytime habitat is improved on streams that are lightly fished because they're too small, too out of the way, or have very limited natural reproduction, my antennae go up, as those projects often concentrate trout without concentrating anglers. By checking out every habitat project you hear about, you'll discover streams that are on the rise action-wise and that the crowds are clueless about.

Chapter 12

Parlor Tricks

I've never liked sitting around and waiting for hatches. That's why prospecting intrigues me—it's an active approach to the sport. It's not about waiting for something to happen so that you can fish to riseforms for a few ephemeral hours. It's about adjusting to the conditions you're dealt and recognizing oddball opportunities, and sometimes it's about making something happen.

CHUMMING

As I worked my way up a brook trout stream on a muggy June afternoon, my nostrils were assaulted by a horrific stench. Something very dead was just ahead and festering in the first real heat of the season. I breathed as little as possible as I fished a long, slow run that was full of brook trout and too good to bypass. Freestone brookies are often suicidal, but these spring-creek squaretails were as skittish as any browns. By the time I'd landed a few, the balance of the trout were zipping up and down the run in obvious agitation. I headed upstream with the intention of getting some fresh air and maybe trying the run again on the way out.

I hadn't walked 30 yards when I saw it—a dead Holstein calf lying half up on the bank with its rump submerged in the stream. I took a deep breath and went in for a look. The body cavity was a writhing, foaming mass of maggots—I could have gone in there with a scoop shovel and filled a 5-gallon bucket. I tied on a cream caddis pupa that was a passable imitation of a blowfly larva, and with the toe of my hip boot, I dislodged a generous dollop of maggots into the drift. As they lined out through a riffle and headed downstream, I hustled back to the run I'd just fished and took six more brookies in quick succession. That was enough for me, although I'm sure the trout would have liked to see the chow keep coming.

Dead animals wind up in and along streams fairly often. Deer, coons, beavers, opossums—anything that's sufficiently ripe can be used to ignite a feeding spree, although, in bear country, it's wise to give ripe carcasses a wide berth. Otherwise, get right in there. It's the stuff that memories are made of.

SHUFFLING BY PROXY

On a steamy July morning, I headed across a cow pasture to look over some spanking new lunker structures. En route, I fished a deep run that's usually good for a few trout, but my nymph came through without a hitch, so I continued upstream and looked at the structures. As I hiked back to the car, I saw a line of cattle crossing at a riffle just above the run I had fished. I kicked it into gear and reached the run just as a payload of silt and churned-up debris clouded the water. And I caught three solid browns—bang, bang, bang—on the same nymph that had been ignored just minutes earlier.

On a May morning, I was nymphing a scooped depression that I knew held some 3-pound browns. I took some smaller fish, but the bigger trout were hunkered down. I was rigging a micronymph and preparing to probe the bottom when a van pulled off the gravel and parked right behind my car. Three fellow fly fishers descended a grassy embankment and fanned out just upstream from me. Other than mucking up the stream with some overly aggressive wading, they did very little on several pretty dependable runs, and then they decided to leave. As they walked downstream toward their vehicle, the pool right in front of me began to cloud in the aftermath of their wading. I detected some flashing in the depths, so I quickly chucked my micronymph in. On the first cast, I hooked a beefy 3-pound brown that put on an aerial show—for an audience of four. I could have kissed that fish.

Long before I ever heard the term shuffling and saw it applied at point-blank range on western tailwaters, I was catching trout in small meadow streams by fishing below watering cattle, which are encountered almost daily on Wisconsin streams. The sudden influx of food into the drift triggers trout to feed actively. And the roiled water makes them less skittish and easier to approach. Anglers who wade like cattle have the same effect. When I encounter this type of disturbance in the course of my fishing, I take advantage of it. Why not? It's payback for the all the times I arrive at a stream only to find the herd bull chewing his cud right next to the one hole I really want to fish, or another angler already there.

MUCK UP THOSE NYMPHS

After you tie on a fresh nymph, jam it right down into the stream bottom and rub some silt into it. That saturates the nymph and removes internal air pockets so that it sinks readily on the very first presentation. It also helps remove any alarming scent.

USE SUN, WIND, AND CLOUDS

When you encounter skittish trout in clear water, you need to take every edge you can get. Tune in to the tempo of the wind and passing clouds. On breezy days, use clouds to eliminate line shadows and wind gusts to disguise line disturbance. On a particularly good fish, wait a bit for favorable conditions and then make your move.

Sun illuminates the shallows, and if you're watching from a high angle, it also illuminates the depths. When the sun is out, take a little extra time to look runs and shallows over from a distance before approaching—it's amazing what you can spot.

THE BAIT AND SWITCH

It happens at some point nearly every season: I hook a chub or a small trout, which is abruptly charged by a big, predatory trout. The big fish may grab the small fish. Or it may swipe at and miss the small fish or simply shadow it. In that event, don't stand there gawking. Get the small fish out of there and switch to a flashy streamer while the big fish is still agitated. There's a decent chance that your streamer will be attacked.

Once you recognize the power of small fish in distress to excite big trout, you can play off of it. When I hook a chub in a big pool that could hide a lunker, I let the chub swim and dart while I peer into the depths for any response or movement. I'll even cast a wriggling chub to the head of a pool and bring it through the deep water. If a big fish shows even momentarily, which is more often the case than a headlong charge, I'll go at him with a streamer. If he doesn't strike, I at least know where he is for another day.

MILK MULTIPLE LEVELS

Often trout distribute to feeding stations in a sort of inverted pyramid, with numerous smaller trout working the upper levels and a few bigger fish foraging deep. That's why it's possible to catch a dozen or more trout from a pool without tapping its potential. Even if you really mop up on active fish at feeding stations, it can pay big dividends to add some split shot and probe deep before moving on.

After fishing a pool for the first time, I'll often wade right through it or loom over it from a high bank and intentionally scatter the fish. I'm taking inventory for my next visit. If I scatter a bunch of trout on a run where I didn't do much, then I know that I need to make some adjustments that day. Of course, if you know what lives in a given run from past experience, then you know whether you've milked it or just scratched the surface.

DOWNSTREAM RELEASE

When small streams are fishing well, individual runs can produce a surprising number of trout, provided you don't stir them up too badly. Steering released fish downstream and away from the run they came out of helps keep a run settled as you continue to work it. On small streams, I often fish runs by standing in or just below the tailout riffles. Trout that are released downstream (behind me) are often reluctant to run upstream through the tailout current and directly past me to get back to their original run. Small fish that are landed quickly and don't require resucitation can be gently pitched—not hurled—downstream a couple feet without injury.

POUND THE RIFFLES

When all else fails, go pound some riffles. Even when the bulk of the trout in a stream are inactive, there are usually a few trout feeding in fast water. And since they must take quickly before food is swept away, trout in riffles are rarely as selective as trout in flat water.

Broken water makes it more difficult for trout to spot you or the impact of your fly line on the surface—two more reasons why riffle trout are relatively easy marks.

SPECIALTY CASTS

In trout fishing, being able to throw the entire fly line comes in handy on occasion. But it's how many different ways, and how accurately, you can deliver a fly inside of 40 feet that matters on most days.

That doesn't mean you should neglect learning to throw a long line. To the contrary. As you work on your long-distance casting, hauling starts to come so naturally that you begin to haul routinely at short distances to generate line speed with a minimum of false casting and to buck wind. The double haul makes you a more accurate and efficient caster, even in tight.

Being able to cast in multiple planes, especially sidearm and over your off shoulder, is imperative.

As a right-handed caster, you can work brushy streams by hugging the left bank and casting sidearm. Casting sidearm also keeps your loops low to the water and under the wind, especially where streambanks are elevated.

On extremely brushy streams, you can eliminate backcasting altogether by letting the line trail downstream and then flipping it upstream with a sidearm cast. As you go into the forward cast, the tension of the line in the water loads the road. Hauling during the forward cast generates extra line speed and distance.

In woods, you can often throw a forward cast away from the stream into an opening in the foliage, and then deliver your backcast to the water.

The drape cast allows you to stay well back from the water and out of sight of the trout. It's a particularly useful presentation on small, clear streams where trout are easily spooked.

(With the correct timing, you can actually turn your wrist so that you're throwing a forward cast in both directions.) In fact, the movement is very similar to the steeple cast, which allows you to cast with your back right up against high trees.

A cast I use a lot on small streams and spooky fish is a drape cast, in which the fly line is draped over land. Casting at a right angle to the stream channel and staying back from the bank can keep you out of sight of spooky fish that just can't be approached. On a drape cast, you need to throw a little extra line to compensate for undulations after the line settles. I particularly like to use this cast with dry flies, because even if I can't actually see the fly, I can sometimes see the disturbance caused by a rising fish, or even hear a rise. To pick up a drape cast without fouling, use a rollcast pickup—that gets the line between the rod tip and the water airborne so that you can snatch the remaining line and the fly off the water.

The tuck cast, which is made by checking the forward cast abruptly and a bit high, causes even a lightly weighted nymph to hit the water with enough force to punch through surface tension and begin sinking immediately. When trout are active and on shallow stations, I often use the tuck cast to slap a nymph on the water to attract attention. On flat water, trout can detect the impact from as much as 10 feet away, and sometimes they'll rush that far to grab the fly. You just have to slap a few casts down (the nymph, not the line) and see how trout respond—aggressively or by fleeing. There are days when trout boil very aggressively to a nymph upon impact.

PART FOUR

Building
a Framework
for Success

Chapter 13

Pacing:
The Neglected Factor

Many aspects of fly fishing have been written about to the nth degree, but I rarely see even a passing mention of pacing. That's a glaring omission, because the speed with which water is covered is fundamental to the success of any angling strategy.

SLOW DOWN FOR INACTIVE TROUT
When trout are inactive, it's best to gear way down and probe a limited amount of water thoroughly—and it should be refuge water where inactive trout stack up. Look for the kinds of places where inactive trout hold, and use the types of subtle presentations that they're most susceptible to, such as micronymphing. It's rare to have really steady fishing for lethargic trout, but if you locate concentrations of fish and work them methodically with slow, subtle presentations at precisely the right depths, you'll enjoy some surprising flurries of action, even when trout are off their feed.

SPEED UP FOR ACTIVE TROUT
Patience is easily the most overrated virtue in fishing. Why do I say that? Because there's no better time to catch trout than when they're active. And the way to make hay when trout are active is to choose an aggressive technique and cover a lot of water. Long-line nymphing, searching freestone rivers with hairwing dry flies, and probing low-density big-fish waters with streamers are all aggressive prospecting tactics that are well suited to catching active trout that are primed to strike on the first presentation.

It's self-limiting to take an aggressive technique and then fish methodically, casting to the same water again and again, yet I see that done routinely; in fact, I rarely see anyone who's not in a drift boat prospecting for active trout at anything approaching an optimal clip. Sure, you might catch an occasional trout on a Royal Wulff on the tenth cast to a given station. But if you take those same ten casts and hit a half dozen stations, and you prospect with that kind of efficiency whenever trout are active, you're going to show your flies to a lot more fish over the course of a season—and many of those trout will pounce on your first presentation.

What's an efficient prospecting speed for active trout? Make one or two good presentations to each station, and then hit the next. If you catch a fish from a slot that could hold several trout, work it a bit more methodically. Otherwise, keep moving. On streams, and even on big rivers, I often prospect more than a half mile of water per hour when trout are active.

Fishing fast doesn't mean walking or wading recklessly. In practice, it boils down to blowing by marginal water and concentrating on the prime runs. When you fish fast, you'll inevitably overrun and spook some trout, especially on unfamiliar water, but if spooking a few trout gets you to a bunch of active trout that you wouldn't have reached otherwise, then it's still a big net gain. And if you spook a really good fish, at least you've discovered its whereabouts for another day. Learn to apply stealth selectively. Being stealthy all the time severely limits your range—and that's a big liability.

This book is about fishing between hatches, but pacing is an equally neglected aspect of fishing during hatches. Assuming you have a reasonably convincing fly and adequate presentation skills, picking up the pace and covering more fish is a sure-fire way to catch more trout during a hatch.

One August, I ran into good pale morning dun hatches on the San Juan River. That entire week, hatches were predictable and fairly heavy. Duns were on the water from noon to around 3 P.M., and plenty of big snouts were showing. By the start of the hatch, I'd be positioned at the bottom of a certain run that was maybe 40 yards long. When fish started rising, I'd work steadily up through the run. If a fish ignored my fly several times, I didn't start switching patterns and get all hung up on him. I just waded right by him and went on to the next fish. By the time I reached the top of the run, fish would be rising again at the bottom. I'd just loop around and cycle back up through the run. During a hatch, I'd wade the entire length of the run a half dozen times. Every day there were other anglers nearby, and basically they stayed put and worked the same water and the same fish for the duration of the hatch. Over the course of the week, I began to recognize and occasionally talk with some of those anglers. They all wanted to see the fly I was using. They assumed that it was the fly, which happened to be a Duck Shoulder Dun no-hackle, that was giving me the hot hand. What they failed to grasp was that I was simply showing my fly to a lot more trout than they were. Incidentally, by my last day on the river, I was down to a few bedraggled Duck Shoulder

Duns, so I switched to a standard Catskill-style hackled dry in a light pale morning dun shade—a style of dun that I didn't expect to do particularly well on that river—and I had my most productive hatch of the week.

When springtime hatches are really popping on midwestern streams, I often walk away from a run while a few fish are still rising and hustle upstream to a fresh run. While the hatch is hot and heavy, I want to show the fly to as many fish as possible. Trying to milk every last riser from a couple of runs can easily eat up 50 percent of my hatch time. That's time better spent on fresh water that's boiling with rising fish.

EXPLOIT NICHES

All trout in a given fishery are not active or inactive simultaneously. That's especially true on big rivers with high fish densities, where trout become specialists. Some routinely nymph deep. Some cruise scum lines or sip midges in quiet back eddies. Some gravitate to the banks to gulp hoppers on hot, windy afternoons. Some root for scuds along weed lines. Where trout feed in specialized fashion, look for active niches of fish. Anytime you identify a niche that can be exploited up and down a river, get on your horse and cover some water before the fish can switch modes.

On fertile tailwaters, exploiting niches means ignoring the bulk of the trout, many of which are visible and very tempting to try for, and focusing on trout that are feeding in a specific fashion. By targeting a select niche of active trout, you're fishing a specific type of water with a single fly at a very efficient clip—and many days you can tear up a river when everybody else is standing around, changing flies, reconfiguring tippets, and working mostly to inactive fish with sporadic results. If you're willing to walk a few miles and fish right through the midday hours, you'll usually find plenty of opportunities to exploit a specific niche, even on the so-called overcrowded tailwaters.

Fly fishing is such a detail-intensive sport that it's easy to get mired in the details and fail to see the big picture. But anytime overall action is slow and you suddenly discover some active fish in a particular water type, you should be asking yourself if that water type is replicated up and down the river. If it is, then get going and check out some similar spots—you'll know in a hurry if you're on to something.

CHERRY-PICK LOW-DENSITY WATERS

For every stream with sky-high trout densities, there are scores of streams with marginal ones. Due to poor natural reproduction, extensive silting, a lack of secure refuge cover, marginal summer temperatures, or a combination of factors, many streams support just a handful of catchable trout per mile. But they can be among the most productive streams to fish—if you attack them efficiently. Not many anglers mess with marginal trout water, and that lack of angling pressure means two things: First, the trout are unsophisticated and very catchable with aggressive prospecting techniques. And second, a disproportionate number of trout are in the upper age classes.

Even on marginal water, there are usually scattered refuge runs that attract the bulk of the trout, but those runs are often a long way apart. On a number of my favorite small streams, I regularly walk 2 miles just to fish a half dozen runs, which means a 4-mile round-trip from the car, but by blowing past long stretches of marginal water, I can work those choice runs in just a few hours. Since land-use patterns, stream character, and fishing pressure are usually consistent within a general area, marginal streams tend to occur in neighboring watersheds, which means you can probably canvass two or three in a day. By prospecting a dozen or more good, neglected runs, you can have some great fishing in complete solitude while other anglers are jostling for position on the popular high-density streams.

Unless a flood rearranges a marginal stream, its holding water can remain remarkably consistent year after year. Once you've been over it a couple times, you know exactly which water to fish and which to skip. The key is to get out there and explore those marginal-looking trout waters, and then cherry-pick only the best runs on repeat visits. If that means walking 10 miles a day, all the better. There aren't many anglers who are willing to walk that far to fish marginal water, and there are fewer still who recognize the upside of doing it strategically. That's why, in this era of stream restoration, I'm happy to see some of those marginal trout waters remain marginal.

Chapter 14

Escaping
Tailwater Crowds

Last September, I spent a week on the Green River below Flaming Gorge in Utah. The Green is one of those famous tailwaters with 5-acre parking lots that fill up with SUVs and driftboat trailers by 9 A.M., even on weekdays. I've fished the Green for a total of about six weeks over the years, but I hadn't been there for five years, and some things had changed in my absence. Right away I noticed that the road to Little Hole, a popular access point 7 miles below the dam, was paved. That struck me as downright progressive until I pulled into Little Hole and discovered that it now costs two bucks a day to park there—and that's on top of the new pass required to use the Flaming Gorge National Recreation Area. And the camping fee had risen from eight to fourteen bucks a night—just for one guy to sleep on the ground. To top it off, the angling traffic was much heavier than I expected it to be after Labor Day, due to an upcoming fly-fishing trade show in Salt Lake. Before I ever stepped into the water, I was wondering if I'd made a mistake in coming here—an apprehension I've felt many times upon arriving at bustling tailwaters.

But I had wonderful fishing, and it was my most enjoyable week on the river to date. One day, I caught better than twenty browns ranging from 16 to 21 inches—and that was just on hoppers when the sun was high. The hopper action sizzled every afternoon and was sandwiched between solid nymphing in the mornings and steady midging in the evenings. As for the crowds, they never cramped my style. In fact, I rarely had another angler within 200 yards.

There's a reason why famous tailwaters are famous—they hold phenomenal numbers of robust trout. And public water that good and accessible is going to attract crowds. Despite all the negative press about overcrowding on the premier western tailwaters, I consistently find fast action and ample elbow room, even during the busy summer months. If you think I'm just desensitized to fishing around crowds, consider that I've made well over one hundred backpack trips to fish off-road waters throughout the Rockies. I'm accustomed to fishing for days at a crack without seeing another human, much less another angler. Yet I still get a big bang out of fishing the great tailwaters. I can fish them on my own for a couple hundred bucks a week, which wouldn't cover the gratuities at most private angling lodges with comparable fishing. And by using my feet and my noggin, I can usually beat the crowds.

There are ways to escape tailwater crowds on these most crowded of all fisheries. Many of these strategies can be applied to other water types, where crowding is less extreme but still significant.

OBSERVE ACCESS PATTERNS AND BE WILLING TO WALK

In summer, a popular tailwater can easily attract several hundred anglers per day. A few dozen anglers hire guides and drift boats and cover significant water. Other anglers have their own drift boats. But most anglers are on foot and unguided, and few of them wander far from popular access points. You can count on one hand the anglers who are willing to walk 5 to 10 miles, but those who do will shake the crowds easily.

For instance, on the Green, 90 percent of the angling pressure originates from just two access points: at the dam and 7 miles downstream at Little Hole. Many drift boats, and recreational rafters, put in below the dam and float to the first takeout at Little Hole. But even though a good trail parallels the river throughout this section, few anglers walk more than 2 miles from either access. One of my favorite strategies is to walk downstream from the dam for 4 miles by early afternoon, and then turn around and fish upstream for the remainder of the day. By evening, most of the drift boats have cleared the upper 4 miles, and most wade anglers are moving back toward the dam, so I routinely work a couple miles of river in virtual solitude.

Below Little Hole, the Green runs through miles of rugged canyon that has no developed trail. Anglers who are willing to hoof over high bluffs and descend to various river sections can fish to trout that see far less pressure than those in the upper 7 miles. I rarely see another wade angler more than 2 miles below Little Hole. Likewise, float use below Little Hole is relatively light and is basically limited to overnight trips, because it's a long way to the next takeout.

On most tailwaters, there are a limited number of boat accesses and definite patterns to drift boat traffic. Observe those patterns and use them to your advantage. In the morning, target water that the drift boat flotilla won't reach until after lunch. In the evening, work water that the drift boats have cleared by late afternoon.

Observing access patterns is also the key to escaping the bulk of foot traffic. The Madison and the upper Missouri both have dozens of miles of productive water, so there I look for areas where the obvious access points are several miles apart, and then walk toward the centers of those sections. In fact, I often bypass the first mile right out of an access so I can spend the bulk of the day on water that sees relatively little pressure.

On tailwaters like the upper Missouri and the Green, which have many productive back eddies and bank-side feeding stations, you can spot plenty of workable fish by walking trails and terraces above the river. By scouting from high vantages, you're able to pattern a river quickly, because you can see where feeding fish station and how they work. As patterns emerge, you can bypass unproductive stretches and target the prime water. When you drop down from a trail or bench, you're not just prospecting blindly—you often have precise fixes on several undisturbed fish.

Walking above a river gives you a bird's-eye view that drifting and wading anglers just don't get. You can spot untapped niches of fish. For instance, as drift boats shoot through rapids, there's little time or opportunity to cast to the banks. Boats usually anchor or pause long enough to work the big eddies below rapids, but they don't row back upstream to work the narrow V of quiet water that often occurs between the inside bank and the head of a rapid. Those are places where I routinely take nice trout by prospecting with drys simply because the drifters aren't burning out that segment of the fish population.

FISH EARLY AND LATE

The famed San Juan River in northern New Mexico draws serious crowds in August and September—the only months I've fished it. Only 4 miles of tailwater are managed under special regulations, and there are numerous access points, so it's not possible to walk completely away from the competition, although there are fewer fish and much less pressure in the lower 2 miles of special regulation water. Within 2 miles of the dam are several parking lots that hold dozens of cars by midmorning. But how many cars are in those lots as dawn streaks over the rimrock? A couple, maybe. Sometimes none. Abandoning a warm bed—or, in this case, a warm sleeping bag—to wrestle into wet wading gear while the stars are still snapping in the cold desert sky doesn't appeal to too many fly fishers. But great fishing is remembered long after discomfort is forgotten, and in the summer, daybreak fishing on the San Juan is memorable indeed.

At first light, I go with 4X and a relatively big, visible fly, such as a Chamois Leech, as I quickly prospect up to a mile of water looking for aggressive fish. With nobody in my path, I can cherry-pick the best-looking water. By the time the sun hits the river, I've usually battled so many big, fat rainbows that my forearm is fatigued—I'll take that kind of discomfort anytime. Even if things really click for me during an afternoon hatch of pale morning duns or blue-winged olives, it's tough to top daybreak prospecting for sheer numbers and size of trout.

By the time the parking lots begin to fill with the after-breakfast crowd, I'm working the far side of the river. It can be 9 A.M. before significant numbers of anglers begin to arrive around me, and by then I've already had four hours of freewheeling. Often I return to the car and eat an early lunch. On the walk back to the car, it's not unusual to see several dozen guys hooking very little on water that was smoking at daybreak.

The last hour of daylight and right into darkness is another window for finding fast fishing and solitude on tailwaters. While many anglers head for the cowboy bars and steak houses before sundown, there's still significantly more competition than you'll see at daybreak. However, the remaining anglers are concentrated within a few hundred yards of access points so they can get off the water quickly at dark. If you set yourself up a mile or more from any access, you can just about bank on solitude during that last hour.

Late evening is a great time to be off by yourself with plenty of undisturbed bank to prospect, because as trout become active, they often gravitate toward the banks. Some of those bank-hugging trout will be big fish that are willing to rise, even if there's no significant hatch. Attractor drys and other sizable flies that were spurned in broad daylight can suddenly begin to click. If you prospect a half mile or more of undisturbed bank in the fading light, you're likely to have some interesting surface action. By dark, cut back to a heavy tippet and throw a big, heavily hackled dry. Even let it drag a bit to create a wake. More than once, I've caught my best dry-fly fish of the day on a big Gray Wulff at 10 P.M.

After a day of intense fishing, I enjoy that long walk out through the sage along a deserted river. It's a time to unwind and to savor the cool of the evening. It's also a two-flashlight job. On moonless nights, it gets so dark, particularly in canyons, that you can't see your hand in front of your face. You can't fish with confidence right into darkness unless you know you have the candlepower to walk out of rugged places. That's why I pack a pair of matching AA flashlights and an extra set of batteries. Each light houses a spare bulb, and all the parts are interchangeable, so it's unlikely I'll wind up without a functioning flashlight.

TARGET MARGINAL DOWNSTREAM WATERS AT MIDDAY

Some of the worst jostling on tailwaters occurs on the prime water during midday hatches. On many tailwaters, you don't need much prime water to yourself when trout are rising, but rather than being hemmed in by other anglers, I often head downstream to where angling pressure begins to dissipate. The fish density is likely to be lower, too, but there are still plenty of trout to keep me occupied, especially if I move from rise to rise during a hatch rather than planting myself in one place.

On the lower half of the special-regulation water on the San Juan, there's an isolated run that's over 100 yards long. For five consecutive years in the early nineties, I fished that run during September *Baetis* hatches. Day after day, I was pretty much alone while anglers were packed together just a mile upriver. At any given time, there were only a dozen or so trout rising on my extensive run, but by stalking from fish to fish and cycling through the run a few times during a hatch, I constantly worked to fresh fish.

Whether you're prospecting or fishing hatches, bear in mind that tailwaters can still provide phenomenal fishing at the point where fish density and angling pressure begin to fall off. Compared with other river types, the density of big fish is still very high. When tailwater trout are active, you may catch more and bigger fish in marginal water than in prime water, because the relative lack of competition gives you the flexibility to move around and target those trout efficiently. And the solitude isn't too tough to take, either.

TARGET TAILWATERS THAT SUIT YOUR STYLE— AND LEARN THEM INTIMATELY

I often fish tailwaters between backpacking trips. I'm typically alone and on foot, and looking to fish on the cheap, which basically restricts me to walking. So over the years, I've targeted tailwaters like the Green, the upper Missouri, the Madison, and the Gunnison, where my willingness to walk works to my advantage. On tailwaters like the Bighorn and the Beaverhead, which have restricted foot access, float fishers hold all the advantages, so I haven't spent much time on those rivers.

Learning a tailwater, or any big river, on your own without a guide is a process. The more time you devote to a river, the quicker you'll develop a working knowledge of it. Even on rivers where I've done well on my first visit, I've continued to learn at a high rate on my next few visits. It takes a month to even begin to understand a big river, and most of us can accumulate that kind of time only over several visits. But with each visit, you learn something about fishing the river and eluding the crowds. You begin to find your own niches, and few things are sweeter than great fishing earned through your own toil and resourcefulness.

Chapter 15

Expanding
Your Universe

Too many anglers fall into the rut of fishing the same handful of waters with much the same tactics throughout the season. But the surest way to elevate your angling success is to expand the number and variety of waters that you fish—and then pick your destination and tactics according to conditions. Usually it's a matter of adjusting to water temperature and seasonal factors, including the location and the mood of trout. The angler who adjusts to those two influences can target the most vulnerable trout on any given day—often right down to a species and age class. But it all hinges on having a diverse inventory of waters to choose from.

If you're fairly new to fly fishing, you'll find that nothing accelerates your learning curve like fishing a variety of water types. Spring creeks, tailwaters, freestone rivers, and lakes are very different habitats that call for different flies and presentations. Every time you tackle a new water type, you learn by leaps and bounds, out of necessity. And what you learn on one water type often transfers to a specific situation on another. For instance, I first learned to micronymph on tailwaters, but I quickly adopted the technique for inactive trout that are bunched into refuge slots on small streams.

Fishing new water on a regular basis also teaches you to quickly recognize water types. And once you grasp the basic nature of new water, it becomes less perplexing and your tactics are more targeted right out of the gate. The very first time I fished Montana's Ruby River, I felt right at home. The Ruby flows through hay meadows and holds mostly wild brown trout. In size, gradient, riffle-run-pool structure, and temperature patterns, it's very similar to some of the larger streams in southwestern Wisconsin. My first day on the Ruby, back in the early eighties, I long-line nymphed with a Soft-Hackle Woolly Worm, just as I often do in Wisconsin, and had fast action for nice browns. I've fished the Ruby a half dozen times in the intervening years, and that fly and tactic have invariably produced my best results.

To develop a large inventory of waters, you have to get into the explorer mode, which can be a lot of fun in itself. In fact, more than anything, it's exploring new water and country that keeps me excited about fishing. As an angler, the world never seems smaller than when I fish the same overworked water repeatedly for diminishing returns. And it never seems larger than when I have a banner day on new water—especially if that water is relatively untapped.

STAY IN TOUCH WITH SMALL STREAMS

Rivers and big streams with good trout fishing are usually well publicized, but small streams are secretive places that you won't read about. You have to discover them on your own. Generally, that means packing a lunch and hiking up that little brook trout stream you've always wondered about, or scouting that neglected brown trout bottom that's overgrown with willows or stinging nettles. If a local stream is classified as a trout water, and sometimes even if it isn't, it merits a few hours of exploring. Even if it turns out that its trout are widely scattered, a stream might still fish well at the right time with the right fly at the right pace, or you may locate a few nice trout that nobody is disturbing.

I try to devote a third of my fishing time to exploring new streams or to streams I haven't visited for a few years. I often explore during marginal fishing times—frosty spring mornings, hot summer afternoons, or even during the closed season when I just feel like walking. As a general rule, what I learn on my first visit to any stream is more important than what I catch. And seeing 2 or 3 miles of water, rather than just a few hundred yards, can drastically change my impression, so I move right along, walking more than I fish. I don't worry about spooking a few trout—in fact, many times I intentionally spook the fish on refuge water just to see what scatters. Whether you're scouting streams, rivers, or lakes, use the sun and high vantages to increase your ability to see deep and spot fish. That allows you to scout a lot of water quickly and efficiently.

By good fortune, and by choice, I live in an area that has dozens of small, fertile trout streams spread over several counties, and the longer I live here, the more I appreciate having so much interesting trout water within an hour or two of my home. Over a season, I typically fish thirty to fifty local streams. Many I visit only once, but the hot ones I return to several times. I make it a point to visit as many streams as I can early in the season, because that clues me to which streams are peaking and leaves plenty of opportunity to cash in. Small-stream fortunes rise and fall quickly; to know of a handful that are fishing exceptionally well, you have to keep a finger on the pulse of dozens. The only way to stay abreast of beaver activity, silting and grazing patterns, flooding effects, habitat-improvement projects, angling pressure, and reproduction trends on dozens of small streams is to get out and walk them. Pay special attention to small streams that have good natural reproduction—those are the streams that can rebound quickly with a single strong year class of fish, especially if habitat improves or angling pressure drops after a number of slow years. By checking such streams annually, you'll catch them on the upswing and enjoy a season or two of fast fishing before others rediscover them. By the way, fishing a lot of small streams doesn't have to involve a lot of driving—one weekend I canvass several neighboring streams, the next weekend I pick a different set.

Several sets of eyes and legs can explore more territory. My brother Eric and his wife, Neysa, fish my home region, so we trade information regularly. If they find an out-of-the-way stream that's fishing like a hatchery race, they call me, and vice versa. Since I know them well, the information I get is reliable. And what we tell each other doesn't go much further.

The rewards for exploring small streams are many. Solitude, sparkling water, and gorgeous native trout often abound. Frequenting small streams makes you a more precise and versatile caster and a better stalker—skills that transfer well to big rivers, which typically fish like small streams when trout move onto feeding stations. And headwater streams are relatively immune to the high water temperatures that severely depress fishing in lower watersheds for much of the summer.

DON'T FORGET ABOUT LAKES

Given a choice, most fly fishers will choose moving water over stillwater, an excellent reason to devote some time and effort to fishing lakes. Granted, moving water is uniquely alluring, but lakes are still plenty intriguing. For starters, trout in lakes often grow larger than those in moving water—and working to big trout always ups the interest quotient considerably.

The remote alpine lakes that dot our western mountains are fascinating to explore and fish. These small, intimate lakes can be fished on foot, using a lot of the same scouting and spotting skills that you employ on moving water. And toting a 50-pound pack over a couple 10,000-foot passes puts you beyond the crowds every time. There is an appropriate payoff for investing that kind of effort: Once you discover an exceptional lake in very remote country, it's like owning private water. You can usually count on great angling for years to come. I've trekked to a favorite golden trout lake in Wyoming more than a half dozen times in the last twenty years, and the fishing is still as superb as it was when I first stumbled onto it. Incidentally, one of the benefits of fishing out of a backpack is that it gets you in shape to outhustle the crowds on hard-fished public waters. I once hiked and fished 150 miles in eleven days across the Frank Church Wilderness in central Idaho. Compared to that, walking 6 or 8 miles a day along a ranch-country river like the Madison is a stroll in the park.

If you're not into hard-core hiking, there are many outstanding and neglected roadside lakes, particularly in the destination areas of the West. It's amazing how fly fishers almost completely ignore even major lake fisheries like Yellowstone Lake, where nice trout and solitude are there for the taking. Even if moving water totally enthralls you, it pays to remember that lakes are more stable environments that often remain fishable when area streams are running warm or dirty.

TRAVEL REGULARLY TO COMPLEMENT YOUR LOCAL FISHING

Argentina, New Zealand, Alaska—I'd love to fish that circuit someday. But meanwhile, I'll settle for less exotic and more affordable destinations that I can fish regularly. It's spending regular time on interesting water that keeps you advancing as an angler and incorporates fishing into the fabric of your life. Whether it's the next state, another region of the country, or beyond, target the best destinations that you can visit annually. Banking it all on the "trip of a lifetime" is invariably disappointing, because no fleeting trip can provide a lifetime of sustenance.

For my budget and inclinations, the Rockies have always been an excellent match. I can fish them on my own for weeks on end for a fraction of the cost of a guided week at a far-flung destination. Over the last twenty-five years, I've managed to fish the Rockies an average of almost two months a summer. Having two young kids has put a serious cramp in my travel time lately, but within the next couple years, I hope to resume traveling for a month or so a year. Since I'll still be on a tight budget, I'm sure I'll head for the Rockies.

The Rockies complement my local fishing, in the Midwest, almost perfectly, and the same is true for anglers who live in the East and the South. In July, when local fishing is slowing down and becoming less inviting, many Rocky Mountain waters are just dropping and clearing after run off, and the best hatches and prospecting conditions are just firing up. In August, when midwestern fishing can really slump, many cold mountain waters are peaking, so I've fished the Rockies more in August than any other month.

I'm also drawn to the Rockies because they harbor a tremendous diversity of water types, including fertile spring creeks and tailwaters, alpine lakes, high plains reservoirs, brawling freestone rivers, tumbling mountain brooks, and quiet meadow streams. The diversity and the sheer amount of good public trout water is unmatched in the Lower Forty-Eight. That's true even before you factor in the millions of acres of backcountry where angling pressure ranges from light to nonexistent. Much of the fishing I do in the Rockies is out of a backpack because that takes me to neglected waters and compelling country. Fishing isn't a competitive sport per se, but unless you can buy your way onto exclusive water, it's important to recognize that today you're competing against scores of anglers every time you string up the rod. And the way to beat the crowds consistently is to outwork them—walk farther, fish longer, fish more strategically and with more intensity. Do what only the few are willing to do, and you'll consistently put yourself on fine water with plenty of elbow room.

Chapter 16

The Advantages
of Fishing Solo

Many of my earliest memories revolve around trout fishing with Dad
and Elmer, my paternal grandfather, riding piggyback as Dad ferried
me across a riffle or sitting in the Red Rooster with Elmer (he named all of
his cars) and dunking my Fig Newtons in his coffee because that's how he
ate them. Before I could read Dick and Jane, I was reading trout water and
wandering off to fish on my own with my Shakespeare Wonder Rod fly rod
and a freshly cut chub tail, one of the all-time great prospecting patterns for
big browns. My brothers, Stu and Eric, were right on my heels in age and
enthusiasm as we fished and hunted for whatever was in season. Today,
whether it's fishing for trout in the hills around home, chasing ringnecks on
the South Dakota prarie, or hunting for big-woods whitetails out of a wall
tent in northern Minnesota, my brothers are still my closest outdoor com-
panions. Good friends, like Duffy Brungardt, have shared western rivers,
mountain trails, and grouse coverts, not to mention all of those deer-shack
dinners of fresh brats piled high with kraut and brown mustard, plus a side
of mean beans—baked beans, onions, and cheese mixed with Tabasco or
leftover chili to give them some snarf. And I hope that my kids, Dale and
Dana, connect with the outdoors.

But for all of those ties, the time I spend alone in the outdoors is often
the most enjoyable. As much as anything, I fish for all that trout connect
me to—wind, rock, water, seasons. For shining mountains of sunlight and
storm. For boyhood streams that still beckon. A little solitude enhances all
of those connections.

And there are many practical advantages to trout fishing alone. I've
talked about expanding your inventory of waters and then picking your
destination and tactics according to conditions. Well, nothing frees you to
make adjustments on the fly like fishing alone. For example, if it turns out

that Saturday is going to be much hotter than was predicted earlier in the week, you can just set the alarm so that you're on the water at daybreak; you're not locked into meeting somebody for breakfast at 8:30. In short, you can make the decisions about when, where, and how you fish based on current conditions—and without a conference call.

When I fish alone, I can use my time more efficiently. If I run out of water, I can blow back to the car and head elsewhere while conditions are still favorable, instead of waiting for a buddy to straggle back an hour later, change socks, and make a sandwich. I don't have to quit early on Sunday evening because somebody else is tired or needs to get home.

As for execution, I almost invariably fish best when I fish alone. Rather than splitting fishing time or water with another angler, I fish full-time without distractions. I find it easier to get into a rhythm and stay there. When conditions are right for running and gunning with an aggressive prospecting technique, then I hustle along and get an undisturbed crack at all the best water. If I see a niche that I think can be exploited, I'm free to follow my hunch.

If you have a solitary streak in your disposition, small-stream angling is the ideal place to indulge it. Putting several people on small water diminishes everyone's productivity. In fact, if I'm fishing a small stream with others, I've already conceded that catching is secondary to companionship on that particular day. That's fine from time to time, but I'm still enough of a diehard that I don't want to fish that way routinely.

Fishing solo also gives me the freedom to explore new water without the pressure to produce fish. If the day turns out to be a complete bust, as exploring often does, I haven't wasted anybody else's time. Yet over time, exploring turns up hot new spots and greatly expands that inventory of waters. And when I do discover an interesting spot on my own, it's mine to milk until I'm ready to divulge it.

Fishing alone also puts me in control of all the peripheral stuff. On overnight or extended trips, I camp simply and inexpensively. I sleep in a small backpacking tent and eat out of a cooler or cans. I can rise before dawn, break camp in ten minutes, and hit the water. Restaurants, hotels, night life, or wrestling with a 40-foot motor home just cuts into the fishing. Besides, I go fishing to immerse myself in the elements, and taking the five-star route or hauling along all the modern conveniences just dilutes the experience. Heck, I routinely cold-camp in the snow while hunting in northern Wisconsin, and there's no more luxurious warmth than burrowing into a down sleeping bag for fourteen hours of darkness while the wind hisses in the pines and the mercury plunges below zero (unless I could talk my wife into a weekend in zip-together bags). Likewise, nothing is quite as snug as a taut, little mountain tent when lightning is bombarding the sur-rounding cirque and rain is lashing by in horizontal sheets. But not every-one likes his nature straight up. At a recent fly-fishing expo, an upscale angler was telling me I hadn't fished Montana until I'd experienced the amenities and the ambiance of a certain exclusive lodge where he spent a week each summer. I came within an eyelash of telling him that he hadn't fished Montana until he'd slept on the ground for about two months straight, but clearly, we were hooked on two different Montanas.

When all is said and done, that's the most engaging approach to fly fishing—not to fish within somebody else's narrow or stuffy definition, but to forge your own fluid style. And there's no better place to begin than by hitting the water with bird-dog intensity every time out—hatch or no hatch.

Bibliography

Borger, Gary. *Designing Trout Flies.* Wausau, WI: Tomorrow River Press, 1991.

———. *Presentation.* Wausau, WI: Tomorrow River Press, 1995.

Born, Steve, Jeff Mayers, Andy Morton, and Bill Sonzogni. *Exploring Wisconsin Trout Streams.* Madison, WI: University of Wisconsin Press, 1997.

Gordon, Sid. *How to Fish from Top to Bottom.* Harrisburg, PA: Stackpole Books, 1955.

Humphreys, Joe. *Trout Tactics.* Harrisburg, PA: Stackpole Books, 1993.

Hughes, Dave. *Essential Trout Flies.* Mechanicsburg, PA: Stackpole Books, 2000.

Mueller, Ross. *Upper Midwest Flies That Catch Trout and How to Fish Them.* Amherst, WI: R. Mueller Publications.

Rosenbauer, Tom. *Reading Trout Streams: An Orvis Guide.* New York: Nick Lyons Books, 1988.

Index

Page numbers in *italics* refer to illustrations.